This book belongs to

_____

...a young woman
who lives for God.

A Young Woman's Guide to Making Right Choices

Elizabeth George

HARVEST HOUSE PUBLISHERS
EUGENE, OREGON

Cover photos © Zave Smith / UpperCut Images / Alamy; Natalia Klenova / iStockphoto

Back cover author photo © Harry Langdon

Cover by Dugan Design Group, Bloomington, Minnesota

A YOUNG WOMAN'S GUIDE TO MAKING RIGHT CHOICES
Copyright © 2009 by Elizabeth George
Published by Harvest House Publishers
Eugene, Oregon 97402
www.harvesthousepublishers.com

Library of Congress Cataloging-in-Publication Data

George, Elizabeth.
   A young woman's guide to making right choices / Elizabeth George.
      p. cm.
   Includes bibliographical references.
   ISBN 978-0-7369-2107-7 (pbk.)
   ISBN 978-0-7369-3196-0 (eBook)
   1. Teenage girls—Conduct of life. 2. Christian teenagers—Conduct of life. 3. Decision
making—Religious aspects—Christianity. 4. Choice (Psychology)—Religious aspects—Christianity.
5. Teenage girls—Religious life. 6. Christian teenagers—Religious life. I. Title.
   BJ1681.G44 2009
   248.8'33—dc22

                                                                              2008053348

Printed in the United States of America

17 18 19 20 21 22 / BP-SK / 21 20 19 18 17 16

Contents

Making the Right Choices

*Choose for yourselves this day
whom you will serve.*

Joshua 24:15

*H*annah was startled out of a deep sleep by the clamor of trash cans being dragged to the street curb. At first she was mad that someone was making all that noise while she was trying to get a little sleep...until she rolled over and looked out her window. It took a bit but she finally realized her dad was doing one of her before-school chores!

"What time is it anyway?" Hannah grumbled. She glanced at the alarm clock. "Oh no, I'm late—way late!"

Maybe it was because she'd pressed the snooze button several times. She'd planned to get up early to finish her English paper that was due today. And there were so many other things to do. She'd planned to do them last night—pick out her school clothes, work on her history paper, catch up on her Bible reading for youth group, write a thank-you note to her grandmother for the birthday money she sent. On and on and on her "Things I Meant to Do" list went.

Yes, Hannah had gotten just a little sidetracked the night

before. And why not? Her best friend had called with terrific news about the new family that had moved in next door to her.

"And guess what! One of the family members is a totally awesome guy who will be in our grade at school," Maria shared.

Hannah knew she would be talking to Maria the next day at school. It wasn't like she would never see her again. After all, didn't they have four classes together? But one thing led to another, and before long Hannah had talked so long (actually an hour past her curfew) that her mom had rudely interrupted and made her end her call and turn out the light.

Life Is Full of Choices

Hannah had every good intention of making right choices about the way she would spend her evening, didn't she? But some one or some thing pulled her away from her plan. In the end—actually the next morning—she suffered the consequences of her bad choices the night before.

Life is full of choices. And the funny thing about a choice is that the same exact choice might be bad for one girl, but OK for another. Take the simple choice of breakfast cereal. Hannah's friend Maria (who wears a size 2) can eat any kind of cereal with all the milk and sugar she wants. But Hannah, who tends toward plump and desperately wants to reduce her jeans size by one or two numbers, has to make a different choice to achieve her goal.

Choices Through the Rearview Mirror

You've probably been to a camp or retreat or youth meeting where there was a "girls' sharing time," a time when girls who were brave enough or sorrowful enough shared some of the not-so-great choices they'd made. It's as if they're looking at their past in a rearview mirror. (If you drive, you know about looking into the rearview mirror to see what's going on behind you, and if you don't drive, you will be one day!) Praise God, the girls who shared in those meetings were now making better... right...choices. But they could still see, remember, and taste the consequences of their actions. Sometimes their language includes these phrases...

- ❋ I wandered off the path...
- ❋ I became a prodigal daughter...
- ❋ I fell away from the Lord...
- ❋ I got sidetracked into sin...
- ❋ I lost my first love...
- ❋ I strayed from the truth...
- ❋ I made some wrong decisions...
- ❋ I went off the deep end...
- ❋ I got in with the wrong crowd...

I've sat in on a few of these sharing sessions, and I can't help but wonder, *What happened? How did someone wander off the path, lose her first love for Jesus, stray from the truth, fall off the deep end, or get involved with the wrong crowd? What specific choices were made?*

Well, we both know what happened, don't we? Some how, at some time, for some reason, a wrong choice was made. Maybe it was just a little lie. Just a little lack of concern for what's right. Just a little bending of a rule. Then little by little these lesser and wrong choices became easier and bigger...until one day a girl realizes her life is a mess.

✎ *From God's Word to Your Heart...*

It's one thing to read a book written by an author about a subject, but it's quite another to read The Book—*The Bible*—written by the Author of all things, God Himself. As we explore God's Word and principles, I'll also be sharing a lot of thoughts and tips to help you. Many of them are things I learned and try to follow, and most of them I passed on to my two daughters when they were growing up. But the things you should truly take to heart and pay attention to are what God tells you in His Word and His Book—the Bible.

When you get to the section in each chapter entitled "From God's Word to Your Heart," you'll find a number of Bible verses on the topic we're discussing. Get out your favorite pen or pencil and mark them up. Don't hesitate to circle certain words or underline things you like. Put a question mark beside anything you wonder about or want to know more about. Even draw in the margins. I've left space for you to write out your thoughts about what God is saying to your heart. Do whatever you like to the verses to help you get their meaning and make them your own. (And, of course, it would be a good choice to look up the verses in your personal Bible!)

The Israelites made a choice. A long time ago, back in biblical times, Joshua, the leader of God's people, asked them to do what we've been talking about—to make a choice. Listen in as Joshua speaks to the people about choosing between serving God and serving false gods. What did they do? Praise God, they made the right choice! They elected to serve God:

> *Fear the LORD and serve him with all faithfulness...choose for yourselves this day whom you*

will serve…But as for me and my household, we
will serve the LORD (Joshua 24:14-15).

How do these verses help you with the decisions you must
make today?

Lot made a choice. Lot was the nephew of Abraham. Because
of their many cattle, Abraham asked Lot to choose between two
parts of the land. One part was perfect for grazing cattle. The
other part was dry hill country and not so perfect. What was
Lot's choice? Sadly, Lot did not choose wisely! He chose the
grassy green pastures, which just happened to be near the two
most evil cities of his day: Sodom and Gomorrah. His choice
was based on what looked good, but the consequences of that
choice were bad—devastating!—for Lot and his family.

Lot looked up and saw that the whole plain of the
Jordan was well watered. So Lot chose for himself
the whole plain of the Jordan and set out toward
the east (Genesis 13:10-11).

How do these verses help you with the decisions you must
make today?

Joseph made a choice. Joseph was sold into slavery in Egypt by his jealous brothers. There, in a strange land, he was a teen-ager without any family. In time, his master's wife flirted with him and wanted him to sleep with her. After all, she probably reasoned, nobody was around. Who would ever know?

What should Joseph do? What *did* Joseph do? He chose to live his life God's way! Joseph honored God and ran from the immoral woman. God honored his choice and made him a leader of the land of Egypt and the savior of his family.

> *But he refused...[and] told her..."How then could I do such a wicked thing and sin against God?"* (Genesis 39:8-9).

How do these verses help you with the decisions you must make today?

Daniel made a choice. Can you imagine being taken as a prisoner to a foreign land as a teenager and told to live by the standards of the land and forsake your religious beliefs? Well, that's what happened to Daniel! In the land of his captivity, Daniel was supposed to eat foods that were forbidden by his Jewish background. What pressure! What did he do? Daniel *chose* to live life God's way, not only on this one occasion, but also many times during his long life. And every step and every day, God blessed Daniel. He was promoted to high positions of leadership.

Daniel resolved not to defile himself with the royal food and wine, and he asked the chief official for permission not to defile himself this way (Daniel 1:8).

How would you use this verse in your life?

Things to Remember About Choices

- Attractive choices sometimes lead to sin.
- Good choices have positive long-term results.
- Right choices are sometimes difficult.[1]

Your Heart Response

I'm sure you know your actions are a matter of choice. Yes, some choices are made for you. They are out of your control and made by those who are responsible for you...such as your parents, your teachers, and your youth leaders. But many choices each day and almost each minute of the day are yours to make. And these choices are a matter of your will. You get to decide what you will or won't do, how you will or won't act. You make the choices and you can't blame anyone else for what happens next.

I enjoyed reading through a teen's journal that was turned into a book. Hear her heart as she comes to the place where she realizes she needs to make better choices:

> *July 29:* It is high time to stop and think. I have been like one running a race and am stopping to take a breath. I do not like the way things have been going lately. I feel restless and ill at ease.[2]

Where is your heart today? And what's happening in your life day after day? Are you confused, unhappy, frustrated, or "restless and ill at ease" as this young woman was? Is it because of the choices you've been making? Please do as Elizabeth Prentiss did and…stop. Evaluate. Make changes. And begin to make right choices.

Things to Do Today to Make Right Choices

❀ Reread the "Choices Through the Rearview Mirror" section. Do any of the comments mentioned in the girls' sharing time fit your life today? If so, talk it over with God. Admit to Him any wrong choices and ask for His wisdom to make right choices starting right now.

❀ Read again Joshua 24:14-15. As you look at your life today, do you think you are making the choice Joshua and his people made—to serve God and God alone? Why or why not? What first right choice will you make to devote yourself to living your life God's way?

❀ Choices are a matter of your will. *You* get to decide what you will or won't do, how you will or won't act. What are you struggling with or facing that calls for better choices from you?

~~~ *Girls Helping Girls* ~~~

❀ Jot down three things Hannah failed to do that started her day down the road to chaos.

❀ What would you tell Hannah to do differently tomorrow to get a better start?

❀ Of the verses shared in this chapter, which one meant the

most to you and why? How would you share that with Hannah?

❀ In what ways are you like Hannah? Are there any new choices you need to start making? What are they? What will you do first?

Want to Know More?
Check It Out!

✓ Read Proverbs 1:10-19. What is the warning given to the young man in verse 10?

What is the advice given to this teen in verse 15?

What is the end result for those who make the choice to participate in evil deeds (verse 19)?

✓ Take a closer look at Lot's choice by reading Genesis 13:5-11. How is the situation described that made a decision necessary (verses 5-7)?

What did Abraham propose as a solution (verses 8-9)?

What choice did Lot make and why (verses 10-11)?

Now quickly scan Genesis 19:12-29. What were some of the results of Lot's choice?

✓ What choice was made by someone in Matthew 4:18-20?

In Matthew 9:9?

Have you made this choice?

God's Guidelines for Making Right Choices

❀ *Treat each day as being important.* "Teach us to number our days aright, that we may gain a heart of wisdom" (Psalm 90:12).

❀ *Admit your need for wisdom…and ask for it!* "If any of you lacks wisdom, he should ask God, who gives generously to all without finding fault, and it will be given to him" (James 1:5).

❀ *Work at developing a deep respect for God.* "The fear of the LORD is the beginning of wisdom, and knowledge of the Holy One is understanding" (Proverbs 9:10).

❀ *Make sure you have a vital relationship with Jesus Christ.* "I keep asking that the God of our Lord Jesus Christ, the glorious Father, may give you the Spirit of wisdom and revelation, so that you may know him better" (Ephesians 1:17).

❀ *Be willing to pay any price for the truth.* "Buy the truth and do not sell it; get wisdom, discipline and understanding" (Proverbs 23:23).

Choice 1

Ya Gotta Get Up!

How long will you lie there, you sluggard?
When will you get up from your sleep?

PROVERBS 6:9

Remember where we left Hannah in the last chapter? In bed! Can you picture the scene—and the sound? Hannah was in a dead sleep. Totally knocked out. And then there was a terrible racket. It took a while for Hannah to realize what that awful clanging was or where it was coming from. As consciousness arrived, she shuddered and thought, *Oh no! That's my alarm…already?* Then she went a step further. *Oh no! Not another day! Ugh!*

Poor Hannah was so tired. (Remember, she'd stayed up late talking to Maria on her cell phone.) *Maybe just a few more minutes?* she thought as she rolled over and pressed the snooze button.

So What's It Going to Be?

Are you looking for a good or better life—a life that's less hectic and more rewarding? Then there's one *really simple* but *really hard* choice you can make every day to help achieve that.

In fact it's the *first* choice to make every day, whether you realize it or not: Will you get up when you need to…or not?

Each morning when your sleep is shattered like Hannah's was…right then and there you make perhaps *the most important choice* you'll make all day. It goes like this: If you get up, you're in control of yourself and your day. (Well, at least you're in control of how it begins. And we have to leave room for God's plan, for interruptions, for crises.) Why can I say that about getting up? Because from Minute #1, *you're* calling the shots. You're in the driver's seat of your day.

As we work our way through this book about your life and your choices, you'll see how this one choice directs or influences the rest of each day. You'll see how Choice #1 affects Choice #2…and #3…and #4… When I was growing up, many of my uncles played dominoes. The game is played by matching the number of dots on one end of a domino with the end dots on another domino. My cousins and I would play with the dominoes when the adults took a break. We didn't know how to play the game so we stood all of the pieces on their ends in a line, one behind the other. If one of us had a shaky hand or bonked the table, all the dominoes toppled, each one tipping the one behind it over. That tumbling of the whole group due to one domino falling is called "the domino effect."

I hate to say it, but when you don't get out of bed when you're supposed to so you can get everything done in an "orderly way" (1 Corinthians 14:40), the domino effect goes into action. *Everything* suffers. It's amazing how that one first choice influences almost every aspect of the day.

Big Results Begin with Small Steps

I like to do things in small steps. It's easier that way, and it makes success and change more achievable. So instead of saying, "I'm going to get up on time or early every day for the rest of my life," I purpose to get up on time for just one day. You see, what you are today is what you have been becoming. And what you are today is what you will be in the future…if nothing changes. Every act repeated—either good or bad—is creating the real you. Each choice—good or bad—made over and over again becomes a habit. And I'm sure your goal (like mine) is to make right choices again and again until you've established good, godly habits.

And, my friend, I'm not talking just about ordinary everyday living here either. Life is so much more than that! For instance, what about your dreams? What do you want to be? What do you want to do? What kind of person do you want to become? Why not write a few of them down?

Well, as they said in the Wild West, "Daylight's a'burnin'!" When you get up in the morning you're grabbing the opportunity to make your dreams come true. You're going to work on becoming the unique person God created you to be and doing the magnificent things He's planned for you. You have all day to make right choices that move you in the direction of something exciting, something excellent, something grand and outstanding, something you can be Christian-proud of at the end of the day.

And when you don't get up? Well, you know all about it!

You miss many opportunities…and often pay a price…to make your dreams happen or move closer to your goal. I like this thought that was in a teen magazine: "Oversleeping will never make dreams come true."[1] And when you get up late and have to rush, you stress out, and your positive attitude for the day turns sour or harried. So getting up is the first right choice you get to make every day. It's a mega-choice!

✎ *From God's Word to Your Heart…*

Keep in mind as you read the following verses that a "sluggard" is someone who has a bad habit of being lazy, slow, or idle. It's someone who hates to get up and hates to work. If you've ever seen a slug on a sidewalk or driveway, you get the picture. Let's take a closer look at "sluggards" to make sure we know who they are. While you read, write down your thoughts on the scriptures and how the principles apply to your life.

> *As a door turns on its hinges, so a sluggard turns on his bed* (Proverbs 26:14).

> *How long will you lie there, you sluggard? When will you get up from your sleep? A little sleep, a little slumber, a little folding of the hands to rest—and poverty [ruin] will come on you like a bandit* (Proverbs 6:9-11).

> ## Sluggards...
>
> ...will not begin things.
> ...will not finish things.
> ...will not face things.[2]

Meet Some People Who Got Up on Time...or Sooner!

As you go through this section feel free to mark up and interact with the verses. These people have a big important message for you and me.

Jesus. God's Son and our Savior, got up early. What did He do once He was awake?

> *Very early in the morning, while it was still dark, Jesus got up, left the house and went off to a solitary place, where he prayed* (Mark 1:35).

Jesus talked to His heavenly Father first thing in the morning. He prayed to God. He received daily strength for doing God's will for one more day. He was spiritually armed for facing and handling temptation, especially the temptation to turn away from going to the cross.

The Proverbs 31 woman. She's a picture of God's ideal woman. Proverbs 31:10-31 is a Hebrew poem, and each verse highlights a character quality. Guess what quality is found in verse 15?

> *She gets up while it is still dark; she provides food for her family and portions for her servant girls.*

This woman was a wife and mom. For her to fulfill one of

God's priorities for her—to take care of her family—she had to set her alarm (so to speak—I wonder what people used back then?) and get up and get going early. Living her life God's way was important enough to get a jump start on the day.

The women at the tomb. Wow! What an example this group of gals is. They loved Jesus. And when He died on the cross, they were there to the very end. Then they followed those who carried their Savior's body to see where He was placed. After that they went home and did the work of preparing spices for Jesus' body so He could be properly buried. And then what did they do?

> *Very early in the morning, the women took the spices they had prepared and went to the tomb* (Luke 24:1).

Do you think they were tired? Do you think it was horrible watching Jesus suffer brutality and die in agony on the cross? And yet these women pressed on with their mission—to tend to Jesus' body and burial. What if they had hit the snooze button on their alarm clocks and gone back to sleep on that all-important morning when they needed to minister to the Lord's body? (Okay, they didn't have alarm clocks like we have, but you get the idea.) What if the women slept in? What if they made excuses and didn't go?

Teens Who Get Up

I'm inspired every time I read about teens who have a passion for something that's so serious and intense that it gets them out of bed. For instance (and this is where your dreams come in!):

My friend's daughter had a horse. She loved that horse like a best friend. She didn't even have to set her alarm at night because she couldn't wait to get up and feed and brush her horse before school. What time did she get up? Five o'clock.

My niece was on an ice skating team. She adored skating. In fact, she slept with her skates in her bed. Guess what time she had to be at the ice rink? Five o'clock. And she had to get up even earlier to get ready and get to the rink on time.

As I'm writing this book, the World Olympic competition is in full swing. I'm sure you've seen the gymnastics competition. Those girls at the Olympic level—most of them in their mid to late teens—are the best in the world. How did they get that way? By training. By practicing. By following instructions. And by getting up early in the morning to do their training... plus their schooling and homework. Each one of these teens was following a dream, a dream powerful enough to get them out of bed each day so they could do all that following—and achieving!—their dreams required.

People get out of bed for all sorts of reasons. To meet with a prayer group or gather for prayer at the school flagpole. To work on a Bible study for youth group. To meet with a study group at school. To go over exam material one more time before the test. To go to sports practice.

What are you passionate about? What do you love doing more than anything else? What do you adore doing but never have enough time for? Take a minute to jot down some answers.

"A journey of a thousand miles begins with a single step." This well-known adage says a lot. For instance, you have dreams and responsibilities that make up your life. So to begin your journey of following and fulfilling your dreams and taking care of your responsibilities, you must begin with one single step—by getting up tomorrow.

1. *What do you want to do tomorrow?* This question has to do with your goals and dreams. In my case I want to purchase a birthday gift for a special friend. My granddaughter wants to have time to sketch in her art pad. Another girl I know wants to practice her driving with her dad before he goes to work so she'll be better prepared for passing her driver's test. What about you? What do you strongly desire to achieve tomorrow? Write it down and note why it's important to you.

2. *What do you have to do tomorrow?* What are your responsibilities? Schoolwork? Work? Chores? Babysitting your little brother? What's on your must-do list? Finishing your term paper? Taking out the trash? Emptying the dishwasher? Feeding the dog next door while your neighbors are on vacation? Take a stab at creating a list. You may need to make it two columns. *Warning:* This list can get quite long!

Your Heart Response

Here's a challenge that really moved my heart. I'm hoping and praying it moves yours too! It's from the book *Don't Waste Your Life*:

> Most people slip by in life without a passion for God, spending their lives on trivial diversions, living for comfort and pleasure…[Don't] get caught up in a life that counts for nothing…Learn to live for Christ, and don't waste your life![3]

Life is a precious gift from God. In addition to the life He's given you, He also has incredible plans and purposes for you. Nothing could be worse than a life that counts for nothing. You have many opportunities to live with passion, make a difference, contribute to others, and bring honor and glory to God. Why not get started today?

Things to Do Today to Make Right Choices

As you think about living your life God's way, let the following choices pave the way for a better tomorrow. This will help you follow through on your first step toward a better life—getting out of bed.

Step 1: Decide when you would like to get up.

Step 2: *Determine when you must get up* to make your day go the way you wish it to go.

Step 3: *Set your alarm*…a good loud one…an obnoxious one!

Step 4: *Get to bed in time* to get the rest you need before getting up on time.

Step 5: *Pray.* Ask for God's help to get up. Tell Him why it's important that you get up on time. Go over your plans, purposes, commitments, and dreams for tomorrow with Him. He cares!

Step 6: *Purpose to get up*…no matter what. Don't give in. And don't worry about not getting enough sleep. It's only for one morning.

Step 7: *Praise God when you hear the alarm.* The psalmist cried out with the dawn, "This is the day the Lord has made; let us rejoice and be glad in it" (Psalm 118:24).

~~~ *Girls Helping Girls* ~~~

❁ What small steps could Hannah take to start her day better?

❋ How do you think Hannah's "Oh no! Not another day!" attitude will affect her day?

❋ Of the scriptures shared in this chapter, which one meant the most to you and why? How would you share that with Hannah?

❋ In what ways are you like Hannah? What do you need to do to have a better approach to the day?

Want to Know More?
Check It Out!

✓ Read Proverbs 6:6-8. What do you learn from the tiny ant that you can remember and copy?

Verse 7 —

Verse 8 —

If the sluggard follows the instructions of verse 6, what will happen?

✓ Read these proverbs and note the results of being lazy.

Proverbs 12:27 —

Proverbs 26:15 —

✓ In Proverbs 26:16, what else do you learn about a sluggard?

✓ Read these proverbs that point out a number of lame excuses offered by the foolish sluggard. Also note the results (or what you think the results will be) of his excuses.

Proverbs 20:4 —

Proverbs 26:13 —

✓ What do you learn about the lifestyle of a sluggard in these verses?

Proverbs 13:4—

Proverbs 21:25-26—

✓ By contrast what does Proverbs 13:4 say is the reward of a diligent lifestyle?

God's Guidelines for Making Right Choices

✻ *Your future starts the second you get up.* "Do not love sleep or you will grow poor; stay awake and you will have food to spare" (Proverbs 20:13).

✻ *Get up...get going...keep going.* "Go to the ant, you sluggard; consider its ways and be wise!" (Proverbs 6:6). "How long will you lie there, you sluggard? When will you get up from your sleep?" (verse 9).

✻ *Realize the value of each day.* "Teach us to number our days aright, that we may gain a heart of wisdom" (Psalm 30:12).

✻ *Have a purpose for each day.* "We constantly pray for you, that our God may count you worthy of his calling, and that by his power he may fulfill every good purpose of yours and every act prompted by your faith" (2 Thessalonians 1:11).

✻ *Look to Jesus as a model.* "Very early in the morning, while it was still dark, Jesus got up, left the house and went off to a solitary place, where he prayed" (Mark 1:35).

Choice 2

Get into God's Word

The law of the LORD is perfect, reviving the soul.
The statutes of the LORD are trustworthy,
making wise the simple.

PSALM 19:7

It's now well past time for Hannah to be getting ready for school. If you remember, we left her pressing the snooze button on her alarm for the third time. Life, as always, has gone right on without her. Everyone at home is up and running… except Hannah.

Her mother comes barging into her room with a very irritated look. She asks, "Why aren't you up and dressed?"

Quick, think fast! Hannah tells herself as she wipes the sleep from her eyes. With an excuse in mind, she blurts out, "There must be something wrong with my alarm clock. I set it [which was true], but somehow it didn't go off [which we know isn't true]. Mom, you need to buy me a new one." For a diversion from the real issue, Hannah argues, "Why didn't you wake me, Mom? You know I have a big day at school!"

Hannah's mom throws up her hands and walks out of the room.

Whew! That was a close one, Hannah decides. As she staggers out of bed, she notices her Bible on the nightstand and the workbook her group is going through. *Oh no! I didn't finish my lesson for tonight's study.* She sighs. *Oh well, no biggie. Right now I've got more important things to deal with. I'm late for school. Maybe I can finish my Bible lesson during history class. Mr. Brown is soooo boring.*

First Things First

I hope right now you're remembering Choice #1, the one that will help you start your day off right. That choice is "getting up at the time you must" to do all the things you want to do and have to do.

Choice #2 is to spend time with God—to have a quiet time with Him. This step will *really* set the tone of your day…and your voice…and your words…and your actions…and your attitudes… and the way you treat people—starting right at home. So once you're up, make God your Number One priority. Choose to put first things first. Meet with Him *before* your day gets rolling.

Sometimes we think we just don't have time to stop and spend time with God. We have people to see, places to go, and things to do. But oh how wrong we are! The Bible is a special book. In fact, it's the greatest book ever written. And if you're a Christian, God's Spirit—the Holy Spirit—speaks to you as you read God's Word. That's why it's so important to take time to read the Bible. When you read it you will think differently. You will live differently. You will grow spiritually. And you will be blessed. These benefits and blessings are worth the effort of getting up a few minutes earlier so you can get into God's Word.

✎ *From God's Word to Your Heart...*

As you read the following scriptures, mark or write down what is said about God's Word and its role in your life.

❀ The Bible keeps you from bad behavior. *"I have hidden your word in my heart that I might not sin against you"* (Psalm 119:11).

❀ The Bible leads you in the right direction. *"Your word is a lamp to my feet and a light for my path"* (Psalm 119:105).

❀ The Bible guides you in the truth. *"All Scripture is God-breathed and is useful for teaching, rebuking, correcting and training in righteousness"* (2 Timothy 3:16).

❀ The Bible prepares you to serve others. *"So that the [young woman] of God may be thoroughly equipped for every good work"* (2 Timothy 3:17).

❀ The Bible sharpens your discernment and judgment. *"The word of God is living and active. Sharper than any double-edged sword...it judges the thoughts and attitudes of the heart"* (Hebrews 4:12)

❀ The Bible gives instructions for eternal life. *"From infancy you [Timothy] have known the holy Scriptures, which are able to make you wise for salvation through faith in Jesus Christ"* (2 Timothy 3:15).

Things to Do Today to Get into God's Word

Wow! Can you see why making the choices to spend time with God and be in His Word are so important? Getting into the Bible and having a quiet time helps you grow in Christlikeness. You become more like Jesus. How does this happen? *It's an inside job!* The Bible changes your heart.

So what can you do to make sure you don't miss out on the miracle of spiritual growth every day? Here are a few steps you can take to get started—or keep going—in getting in Bible time. When you take these steps each day, you're choosing to make time with God a priority—your #1 priority!

Step 1: *Read God's Word.* Start anywhere. The only wrong way to read the Bible is not to read it. If you don't know where to begin, start in Matthew and read the four Gospels (Matthew, Mark, Luke, and John).

Step 2: *Study God's Word.* Dig deeper into your Bible. If you're not sure how, ask someone for help.

Step 3: *Hear God's Word.* Make sure you go to church and get into youth group so you'll hear God's Word taught and explained. You want to understand all you can!

Step 4: *Memorize God's Word.* There is no better way to live God's way than to have His Word in your heart and mind...and follow it. If it's there, He will use it in your life.

Step 5: *Desire God's Word.* You already know the importance of physical food. Well, you need to see the spiritual food of the Bible as having even greater importance. Job declared, "I have treasured the words of [God's teaching] more than my daily bread" (Job 23:12).

The Best Kind of Studying

If you're a Christian, it makes sense that you want to learn as much as you can about Jesus Christ and His Word. Think about it—of all the things you learn in your life, what's the most important? And it's not algebra or biology. Although studying those subjects is important and necessary, the most important thing is to know who God is and what He wants you to do in your life. The more you learn about Him, the more you'll feel secure and have strength for the challenges you face now and in the future. Reading the Bible is the best kind of studying![1]

KELLI

A Word About Memorizing Scripture

If you're like most teens, you have no problem memorizing the lyrics to your favorite songs. I see girls listening to music all the time. I hear them singing as they're walking down aisles in stores or on the street. The words are there, working on their minds and coming out of their mouths. Well, that's how easy and natural memorizing God's Word can be...*if* you choose to make it part of your life.

God told Joshua to meditate on His Word day and night (Joshua 1:8). This means God expected him to know His Word by heart! The Bible also tells young men and women to "hide" God's Word in their hearts that they might not sin against Him (Psalm 119:11). God sees His Word in the hearts of people as a safeguard against sin, wrong choices, and the pain and shame that often go along with making poor or wrong decisions.

The young teen woman, Mary, who became the mother of Jesus, our Savior, was passionate about memorizing portions of the Bible. How do we know this? Mary treasured and pondered God's Word in her heart because when she opened her mouth to praise God for the blessing of the Savior, out came Bible verses (Luke 1:46-55)! She made at least 15 references to scriptures from the Old Testament! Mary obviously had memorized these verses and truths on purpose (a great choice!). She learned them by heart, and they became her language. Truly, when she opened her mouth, her lips spilled God's Word. And it was His Word in her heart that helped her embrace and live God's plan for her to become Jesus' mother.

Here's a special assignment for you. What is your favorite verse in the Bible? Write it down and memorize it. Make it your own. And if you can't think of a verse, use one of the two on the next page.

My favorite verse is:

Be strong and courageous. Do not be terrified; do not be discouraged, for the Lord your God will be with you wherever you go (Joshua 1:9).

In all your ways acknowledge him, and he will make your paths straight (Proverbs 3:6).

Your Heart Response

Just think—the Bible is all yours all the time. And it's the ultimate beauty treatment. God's Word makes its way into your heart and lifts your soul. It changes your views about people and the things that are happening in your life. Do you want a better life? You can have it! Your better life is as close and as easy as making the choice to open your Bible each day and taking a few minutes to read and soak up God's love letter to you.

~~~ *Girls Helping Girls* ~~~

❋ What can you tell Hannah about the importance of meeting with God and the difference it can make in her life? How do you think her behavior might change?

❋ Of the verses shared in this chapter, which one meant the most to you and why? How would you pass that on to Hannah?

❋ In what ways are you like Hannah? Are there any new choices you need to make? If so, what are they? What will you do first?

Want to Know More?
Check It Out!

✓ Read Psalm 19:7-10. Note the different terms used for the Bible in each verse. Write down how it's described and its effects on those who read it.

	Term	Description	Effect
Verse 7			
Verse 8			
Verse 9			
Verse 10			

✓ In verse 11, what benefits belong to the one who listens to and keeps God's Word?

✓ Read Joshua 1:7. What are God's commands regarding His Word? (As you read, remember that *success* is God's blessings lavished on you because of your obedience. He blesses you when you live your life His way.)

-

-

When you do as God says, what will you experience?

✓ Now read Joshua 1:8. What are God's commands regarding His Word?

-

-

-

When you do what God says, what will you experience?

God's Guidelines for Making Right Choices

✤ *The Bible keeps you from sin.* "I have hidden your word in my heart that I might not sin against you" (Psalm 119:11).

✤ *The Bible leads you in the right direction.* "Your word is a lamp to my feet and a light for my path" (Psalm 119:105).

✤ *The Bible answers your questions.* "All Scripture is God-breathed and is useful for teaching, rebuking, correcting and training in righteousness" (2 Timothy 3:16).

✤ *The Bible gives you discernment.* "The word of God is living and active. Sharper than any double-edged sword, it penetrates even to dividing soul and spirit, joints and marrow; it judges the thoughts and attitudes of the heart" (Hebrews 4:12).

✤ *The Bible is your ultimate treasure.* "The precepts of the LORD are right, giving joy to the heart. The commands of the LORD are radiant, giving light to the eyes... They are more precious than gold, than much pure gold; they are sweeter than honey, than honey from the comb" (Psalm 19:8,10).

Choice 3

Talk Things Over with God

In everything, by prayer and petition,
with thanksgiving,
present your requests to God.

PHILIPPIANS 4:6

allelujah! Hannah's up! *Whew!* As she stands up, the first
thing she sees is her Bible and her unfinished Bible lesson
on the nightstand. "Oh no!" she groans as she realizes she's failed
miserably in fulfilling her commitment to pray every day this
week. She hadn't really wanted to make that commitment, but
her friends in the church group had been so excited that she'd
gone along with them. They were studying about prayer, and
they had wanted to put what they were learning into practice
by pledging to pray.

"What was I thinking? I can't believe I did that!" Hannah
muttered. "What a waste of time. Everything's going great in my
life. Why do I need to pray? And for who...and what? Missionaries I don't know? Sick people? And sure, family's important,
but I'm not so sure about praying for Jason and Tiffany. Even

though they're my brother and sister, they're such a pain. But I did say I would. OK, God. Here goes. *Bless the missionaries and my family today—even Jason and Tiffany. And, of course, bless me! Amen."*

> *God calls us to pray and think and dream*
> *and plan and work not to be made much of,*
> *but to make much of Him in every part of our lives.*
>
> JOHN PIPER

God Is Available to You 24/7

"Is that your cell phone ringing?" We hear this every day, don't we? Everyone seems to have a cell, and there are very few places where you can't receive a signal. In many ways prayer is like a cell phone. You can pray anytime you want, anywhere you want, for as long as you want. But unlike a cell, prayer has no fees or roaming charges. You also never have to scroll through a directory to find God's number. And your communication with God requires no earpiece—it's hands free. Plus you have a direct line to the God of the universe 24/7—24 hours a day, 7 days a week. How's that for technology? Divine technology, that is!

10 Reasons We Don't Pray

With the details of prayer being as easy as bowing your head and simply talking your life over with God, you'd think we'd pray a lot more than we do. Have you ever thought about why you don't pray more? As I look at my own heart and life, I've discovered some reasons—and excuses—I have for not praying. See if you can relate.

1. *Worldliness*. Our world affects us more than we think. It exerts a constant pressure on us to conform and live like the world lives...instead of living God's way. And because we have food, clothing, shelter, family, friends, and lots of fun things to do, we wrongly think, *Why do I need to talk to God? I've got everything I need without praying*.

2. *Busyness*. Like Hannah, we often don't take the time or make an effort to pray. Prayer isn't a priority, so we fill our hours with seemingly more important things. We're so busy we don't even get around to thinking about how to fit praying into our daily lives.

3. *Foolishness*. When we're consumed with what's foolish, trivial, and meaningless, we fail to pray. We lose our ability to know the difference between what is good and what is evil, between what is essential and that which has little eternal value. Everything becomes a "gray area" that doesn't require prayer (or so we think).

4. *Distance*. We have no problem talking with our friends. Why, Hannah and her friend Maria talk for hours! But talk to someone outside our social circle? Forget it. And it's the same with talking to God. When our relationship with God isn't a personal one, we find it hard to talk to Him. We don't know what to say and we don't feel close to Him or comfortable in His presence, so we don't share our real selves with Him.

5. *Ignorance*. We're clueless about how prayer works. And we

don't understand how it helps or fits into our relationship with God and making right choices. In essence, we really don't understand God's love for us and His power to make our lives better.

6. *Sinfulness.* We don't pray because we know we've done something wrong. In our hearts we know we need to talk to God about it, confess it, and agree with Him that what we did is wrong. What can we do about our sins and failures? Make a choice to keep short accounts with God. Deal with any sin when it comes up—right on the spot—at the exact minute we slip up and fail.

7. *Faithlessness.* We don't believe in the power of prayer. Often it's because we don't know or realize the power of the dazzling promises God has made to us. We don't know about His assurances that He'll hear and answer our prayers. We don't think prayer makes any difference, so we don't even try.

8. *Pride.* Prayer shows our dependence on God. When we fail to pray, in our pride we're saying we don't have any needs. Or worse, we're saying, "God, I'll take care of the situation and me. I don't need You right now."

9. *Inexperience.* We don't pray because…we don't pray. And because we don't pray, we don't even think to pray…so we don't. We're like a dog chasing after its tail. It's a cycle that leads nowhere.

10. *Laziness.* Maybe this is the chief obstacle. We won't put out the effort to talk to God. We don't want to take the time. Prayer is an act of the will. It's a choice. We have to want to do it…and then *choose* to do it.[1]

✎ *From God's Word to Your Heart...*

As you read each of these sparkling promises and assurances about prayer, note God's message to your heart regarding your life and how prayer helps you live it His way.

> *"Call to me and I will answer you and tell you great and unsearchable things you do not know," [says the LORD]* (Jeremiah 33:3).

> *Love your enemies and pray for those who persecute you* (Matthew 5:44).

> *Whatever you ask for in prayer, believe that you have received it, and it will be yours* (Mark 11:24).

> *Let us then approach the throne of grace with confidence, so that we may receive mercy and find grace to help us in our time of need* (Hebrews 4:16).

> *If any of you lacks wisdom, he should ask God... and it will be given to him* (James 1:5).

Is any one of you in trouble? He should pray (James 5:13).

If we confess our sins, [God] is faithful and just and will forgive us our sins and purify us from all unrighteousness (1 John 1:9).

You do not have, because you do not ask God. When you ask, you do not receive, because you ask with wrong motives, that you may spend what you get on your pleasures (James 4:2-3).

Your Heart Response

Prayer is a spiritual activity, and it takes a heart decision and requires effort. So if you're not praying—or not praying very much—run through this checklist:

❀ *Check your relationship with God.* Is there something that's caused a barrier between you and God? If so, bow your heart and admit it to God. Ask Him to help you do whatever it takes to deal with the obstacles that stand between you and a loving, open relationship with God, one that enables you to talk to Him about anything and everything...including making right choices.

❈ *Check your lifestyle.* What...or who...is influencing you? Are you being influenced positively for the things of God? If not, it's out! Nothing and no one is important enough to endanger your relationship with God and your willingness to talk to Him in prayer.

❈ *Check your desire.* Prayer will never become a wonderful habit or spiritual discipline if the main ingredient—desire—is missing. We can know what to do and why to do it, but if we don't want to do it, it won't become real in our lives.

My friend, do you want to pray? I believe you do! Here are two simple principles (more great choices!) that will help move you forward in defeating or overcoming your excuses for not praying.

❈ *Principle #1*—Head to bed. You want to fulfill Choice #1, don't you—to get out of bed on time tomorrow morning? Well, it starts by thinking about getting ready for bed early in the evening. Finish your homework. Do all your pre-bed stuff—wash your face, brush your teeth, and so forth. Then check your schedule and create a "to do" list for the next day. Set out your Bible and prayer notebook in a place where you will have your quiet time the next morning. And then go to bed—early—so you can meet and talk with your heavenly Father in the morning.

Did you know sleep experts say you need eight-and-a-half to nine-and-a-quarter hours of sleep every night? "Yet the overwhelming majority of teens (85 percent) get less than that—on average, about two hours less. The result is that most of today's teens are chronically sleep-deprived. Many are so sleepy that they live in a kind of 'twilight zone.'…the term 'zombie' is a pretty accurate description."[2]

❀ *Principle #2*—"Something is better than nothing." Any prayer is better than no prayer. Some prayer is better than none. Start with a choice to pray a few minutes each morning. Graduate little by little to more time spent in prayer.

~~~ *Girls Helping Girls* ~~~

❀ Jot down two or three excuses Hannah had for not praying. Also note some of her bad attitudes.

❀ What can you tell Hannah about the importance of prayer and the difference it can make in her life? What can you tell her about the difference prayer has made in your life?

❀ Of the scriptures shared in this chapter, which one meant the most to you and why? How would you pass that scripture on to Hannah?

❋ In what ways are you like Hannah? Are there any choices you need to start making about prayer? What are they? What will you do first?

Want to Know More? Check It Out!

✓ The Bible is filled with people who made the choice to pray about their lives and choices. See what you can learn about the difference prayer made in these Old Testament people's lives and what they talked over with God.

David—read Psalm 32:1-5. What was the issue in David's life, and how did prayer make a difference?

Abraham—read Genesis 18:20-33 and 19:29. What was Abraham's concern and what did he do about it? And the results?

In the New Testament we learn much from Jesus, who prayed perfectly. Read Luke 6:12-13. How long did Jesus pray, and what decision did He make afterward? Also jot down the decisions you're facing and then note on your calendar a time you will pray about them.

Now read Matthew 26:36-46. What was Jesus' intention (verse 36)?

- How is the seriousness of Jesus' situation described (verses 37-38)?

- What was Jesus' posture when He prayed (verse 39)?

- Jesus was praying about the "cup" of death on the cross. How many times did He pray about doing God's will (verses 39-44)?

- What was Jesus' overwhelming desire—what He wanted above all else—that was repeatedly expressed in His prayers in Gethsemane (verses 39, 42, and 44)?

- After extended time in prayer, how did Jesus respond to God's plan for Him (verse 45-46)?

Nehemiah's Prayer Life

- When discouraged, he prayed (Nehemiah 1:4).
- When seeking direction, he prayed (1:5-11).
- When seeking assistance, he prayed (2:1-5).
- When under attack, he prayed (4:4-5,9).
- When weak and powerless, he prayed (6:9).
- When joyful, he prayed (12:27,43).[3]

God's Guidelines for Making Right Choices

❀ *Walk in obedience to God's Word.* "If anyone turns a deaf ear to the law, even his prayers are detestable" (Proverbs 28:9).

❀ *Bring all your concerns confidently before God.* "God has surely listened and heard my voice in prayer. Praise be to God, who has not rejected my prayer or withheld his love from me!" (Psalm 66:19-20).

❀ *Remember to pray in times of trouble.* "The eyes of the LORD are on the righteous and his ears are attentive to their cry…the righteous cry out, and the LORD hears them; he delivers them from all their troubles" (Psalm 34:15,17).

❀ *Replace your worry with prayer.* "Do not be anxious about anything, but in everything, by prayer and petition, with thanksgiving, present your requests to God. And the peace of God, which transcends all understanding, will guard your hearts and your minds in Christ Jesus" (Philippians 4:6-7).

❀ *Cultivate prayer as a ministry.* "Pray in the Spirit on all occasions with all kinds of prayers and requests. With this in mind, be alert and always keep on praying for all the saints" (Ephesians 6:18).

Choice 4

The Golden Rule Begins at Home

Do to others as you would have them do to you.

LUKE 6:31

Watch out! Hannah's on the move! She's finally out of bed—very late. She's already had a tiff with her mom and now she's on the loose. As she tromps down the hall to the bathroom, the world awaits her, starting with her little brother, Jason, and her little sister, Tiffany.

What a big pain! Hannah thinks when she sees Jason.

Jason is three years younger than Hannah and always makes a complete pest of himself, especially when Hannah's friends come over.

Ugh! There's Tiffany. She sure thinks she's a princess—and acts like it too.

Hannah's day isn't starting off well at all.

Tiffany is 10 and already likes to get into Hannah's stuff and "borrow" Hannah's clothes.

Hannah thinks one of her callings in life is to find ways to make Jason and Tiffany miserable. And here comes her first opportunity today.

"Get outta my way or you'll be sorry!" Hannah barks at both of them. "And get outta the bathroom! Can't you see I'm late? Give me some space!"

Hannah muscles her younger siblings out of the bathroom, slams the door in their faces, and locks it. Sure enough, Hannah's poor brother and sister got the brunt of her waking-up anger. They have to get ready for school too, so they bang on the door and yell for Mom to come to their rescue.

Is Hannah living a charmed life? First she dodged taking out the trash (mmm, good ol' Dad!). Next she manipulated and lied to her mom to escape being grounded. And now she's bullying her brother and sister out of the bathroom with harsh words, muscle, and threats. "I'll show them who's the *real* princess!" her attitude shrieks.

✎ *From God's Word to Your Heart...*

I'm sure you've heard of "the Golden Rule." Did you know Jesus was the One who said it first? He did! "These verses are commonly known as the Golden Rule. In many religions, it is stated negatively. '*Don't* do to others what you *don't* want done to you.' By stating it positively Jesus made it more significant. It is not so hard to refrain from harming others; it is much more difficult to take the initiative in doing something good for them. The Golden Rule as Jesus formulated it is the foundation of active goodness and mercy—the kind God shows to us every day."[1] As you read these two quotes from Jesus, mark what stands out to you.

*In everything, do to others what you would have
them do to you, for this sums up the Law and the
Prophets* (Matthew 7:12).

Do to others as you would have them do to you
(Luke 6:31).

Who You Are at Home Is Who You Are

I truly live by the truth that "who we are at home is who
we are." When my daughters were growing up, I reminded
them of this truth too. Why would a Christian act one way out
in public—at school, at church, at work—and another way at
home? Why would a Christian behave one way with friends and
another way with family? They shouldn't!

The word for this kind of dual behavior is *hypocrisy,* which
comes from the noun *hypocrite.* It means "phony." A hypocrite
is a deceiver, a play-actor, a pretender. Someone who puts on
a mask and pretends to be what he or she isn't. It's being one
kind of person to some people, and then being the opposite
kind of person to others.

Have you heard the term *two-faced?* Well, it's the same thing.
And have you known someone who was two-faced, who played
the part of two different kinds of people? (Or…gulp…have *you*
acted in a two-faced manner?) Do you remember how nice
Hannah was to her friend Maria? They happily talked on the
phone for a long time. But now we see how Hannah treats her
brother and sister. She is two-faced. She acts out two roles. She's

a modern-day Dr. Jekyll and Ms. Hyde. To her family she's mean and ugly. But with her friends Hannah turns sweet as honey.

✎ *From God's Word to Your Heart...*

Sometimes we can learn a lot about actions by studying their opposites. How do these scriptures speak about actions opposite Hannah's behavior toward her family? And how are you doing in these areas?

> *Be kind and compassionate to one another* (Ephesians 4:32).

> *Be imitators of God, therefore, as dearly loved children and live a life of love* (Ephesians 5:1-2).

> *The fruit of the Spirit is love, joy, peace, patience, kindness, goodness, faithfulness, gentleness and self-control* (Galatians 5:22-23).

Christ Transforms Us from the Inside Out

Have you noticed that many of the choices we've been talking about involve your heart? Basically they involve *loving* God, *learning* what He says about the issues of your life, and then *following* His principles…making the right choices and decisions based on what His Word says and prayer.

And the choice to practice the Golden Rule is no different. The way we talk to others and treat others is a heart issue. Why do I say that? Because Jesus said it. Here's how it works: "Out of the overflow of the heart the mouth speaks. The good man brings good things out of the good stored up in him, and the evil man brings evil things out of the evil stored up in him" (Matthew 12:34-35).

Do you remember what your life was like before you became a Christian? Can you recall how you acted toward others? How you treated people? Even when you were being nice you couldn't love as much as you can now that Jesus is in your heart. The Bible says you were dead in your sins, that you were controlled by the forces of evil. Your actions conformed to a heart of unbelief (Ephesians 2:1-3).

But thank goodness God didn't leave us there! The Bible reveals that God, in His great love, showed mercy toward you and me, making us alive with Christ: "By [God's] grace you have been saved" (Ephesians 2:5 NKJV). By God's grace we were also transformed—changed—from the inside out. We are now new creatures in Christ (2 Corinthians 5:17). So live out what God has put into your heart! Live out the actions of the Holy Spirit. (Look again at Galatians 5:22-23 to review the list of godly actions.)

Choices for Living the Golden Rule

1. *Choose to have a heart checkup.* Are you fed up with the way you're living your life? With the way you've been treating people? Ask Jesus to escort you through a spiritual checkup. Ask yourself, *Has my heart been transformed by God from the*

inside out? Is Jesus really my Savior? Have I truly submitted my life to His leading?

If you answer "no" to any of these questions, you are still spiritually dead. Your condition requires a complete spiritual makeover…from the inside out. And only God can do that! So start now. Ask Jesus to come into your heart and your life. You need life as only He can give it—*spiritual* life. The only way to live like Jesus and abide by His Golden Rule is to invite Him to be your Lord and Savior. This simple, earnest prayer can open the door of your heart to Christ and to a transformed life. Jesus into your heart…and you'll be transformed!

> *Lord Jesus, I don't know You as my Savior. I am separated from You because of my sins. Forgive me. Come into my life right now and take control of my actions. I want to follow You. I want to love others with Your love. I want to be kind. I want all of the godly qualities You list in Your Word and lived out in Your life. Help me turn from my sins and follow Your example and love others as You love me. Amen.*

Talk to God. And then talk to someone who can help you know Jesus and grow to be more like Him.

2. *Choose to revisit your heart.* If Jesus is your Savior, you have His Spirit living in you. This means you have the ability to be nice to all people, to treat others the same way Jesus did. So what's the problem? Why doesn't this happen? Answer: *unconfessed sin.* Sin is like filth in a water pipe. Dirt and garbage clog it up, keeping water from flowing freely. That's how sin works. Sin clogs the Holy Spirit's flow through you. But if you choose to confess your sin and repent, allowing God to clean out your dirty pipes, you can live your life God's way (1 John 1:9).

3. *Choose to read your Bible.* The Bible has the power to work spiritually in your life from the inside out. When you make the second choice (after getting up) of your day by reading from the Bible, you're not the same. God's Word is pure, powerful, life-changing, and spiritual. When you read it and allow it to change your heart and mind, you no longer think or act in worldly or bad ways. As you get into God's Word you'll discover His Spirit transforming you (Romans 12:1-2). The more you read, the more you grow, the more you become like Christ! Treating others in a kind and Christlike way becomes easier.

4. *Choose to be nice at home.* It may be hard to believe or swallow right now, but there is nothing like family. Friends come and go. Some are fickle and turn on you. Others move away... or move on to new groups. But your family is forever. One year, five years, ten years and more from now you'll still have your family. So why not invest the bulk of your kindness and good-ness at home? That's where the people who matter the most to you are. Yes, even your noisy, nosy, nuisance brothers and sisters. Try these simple kindnesses. You'll be amazed at what a difference it makes in your life and theirs!

❋ Choose to give a cheerful hello in the morning.

❋ Choose to give a compliment every day.

❋ Choose to help your little sister clean up her spilled milk or brush her hair.

❋ Choose to help your little brother find his backpack.

❋ Choose to help Mom on a project without being asked.

❋ Choose to help Dad on a project without being asked.

Remember, who you are at home is who you are. In my book *A Young Woman After God's Own Heart*, I shared about the importance of going through life as *givers,* not *takers:*

> Imagine that you are the richest person in the world. It's in your power to bless everyone else in the whole world because you have so much to give and share with others. Then imagine yourself walking down a path or a road or a street (or a corridor at school—and let's add the hall at home!). And there you are...literally throwing your riches away, exuberantly tossing them to everyone you meet. You smile! You greet them! And you give them something![2]

Choose to be a giver and start where it counts the most—right where you live. Give to those you live with. It's like this. If you can do it at home, guess what? You can do it anywhere! If you can give to family, guess what? You can give to anyone! Why? Because who you are at home...and you know the rest!

Remember what the young woman mentioned in the introduction wrote in her journal about the Golden Rule: "I can now choose to imitate my Master, who spent His whole life in doing good."[3]

Your Heart Response

Don't you love it when people practice the Golden Rule and are nice to you? It's a great feeling. Unfortunately, you and I don't always pass the Golden Rule treatment on to others, especially when it comes to family. How many times has your mom or dad told you, "Be nice to your brothers and sisters"? Probably more times than you want to admit, right? Here's an interesting truth: Did you know that the Bible never tells us to "be nice"? But wait! Before you run off to share that, let me explain. What the Bible *does* say is that we're to "be kind" (Ephesians 4:32).

What's the difference between being nice and being kind? Nice is just being polite, but kindness is caring and being thoughtful. Kindness involves being compassionate and considerate. Nice is superficial. We can "act" nice toward someone even when on the inside we can't stand him or her. But kindness is different. It's a deep, intense, heartfelt action. It requires heart—*our* hearts. And God will help us be kind—even to our not-so-favorite people.

Won't you please allow God's Spirit to move your heart and choose to be kind? Opt to practice God's Golden Rule everywhere, especially at home. Just think what it will mean to those in your family. They will be blessed. And best of all, God will be honored by your actions.

Girls Helping Girls

❀ Jot down two or three ways Hannah mistreated her family members. Also note some of her attitudes.

❀ What would you tell Hannah about why and how she should practice God's Golden Rule at home?

❀ Of the scriptures shared in this chapter, which one meant the most to you and why? How would you pass that on to Hannah?

❀ In what ways are you like Hannah? Do you need to make any new choices concerning your own family...and people in general? If yes, what are they?

Want to Know More?
Check It Out!

The Bible has much to say about "doing to others what you want done to yourself." These are often referred to as "the one anothers."

✓ Look up and note the "one anothers" in the following scriptures. Jot down how you will start applying them in your relationships. First focus on your family, and then move on to your friends and acquaintances...and even those who may be, in Jesus' words, "your enemies" (Matthew 5:44). (Be alert: Some verses contain more than one.)

Romans 12:10—

Romans 12:16—

Galatians 5:13—

Ephesians 4:2—

Ephesians 4:32—

1 Thessalonians 5:11—

James 4:11—

John 13:34—

God's Guidelines for Making Right Choices

✿ *Guard against anything that would divide you from your family.* "How good and pleasant it is when brothers live together in unity!" (Psalm 133:1).

✿ *Concentrate on being a helper.* "She gets up while it is still dark; she provides food for her family and portions for her servant girls" (Proverbs 31:15).

✿ *Develop a team mentality.* "Two are better than one, because they have a good return for their work: If one falls down, his friend can help him up. But pity the man who falls and has no one to help him up!" (Ecclesiastes 4:9-10).

✿ *Show love to your family.* "Whoever loves his brother lives in the light, and there is nothing in him to make him stumble. But whoever hates his brother is in the darkness" (1 John 2:10-11).

✿ *Accept God's plan of obedience.* "Children, obey your parents in the Lord, for this is right. 'Honor your father and mother'—which is the first commandment with a promise—'that it may go well with you and that you may enjoy long life on the earth'" (Ephesians 6:1-3).

Choice 5

"I Have Nothing to Wear!"

Whatever you do,
do it all for the glory of God.

1 Corinthians 10:31

Finally forced to vacate the bathroom by a host of family members, Hannah moved down the hall to her room in a huff.

"Someday," she mutters, "I'll get out of here and have my own apartment. Then I'll be able to take as long as I want in the bathroom." As she opens her bedroom door with the bold "Keep Out or Die!" sign on it, she wonders, *Now let's see...what to wear?*

Entering her room is like going into a disaster zone! Clothes, books, CD cases, unfinished projects, and trash are strewn everywhere. *No big deal,* she decides. *I'm late for school. I'll clean up my room some other time.*

Sidestepping several piles, Hannah approaches her closet. As she opens the sliding door, an avalanche of stuff, including dirty clothes, cascades out. Unfortunately this means there isn't much of a selection of clean clothes left. Thinking about her times at Maria's house, Hannah sighs. *Why don't I have a mom like Maria's? Mrs. Ortiz is so cool! She washes Maria's clothes and keeps her room picked up. And Maria always has lots of clean clothes to wear. Her mom even makes sure Maria has the latest fashions! And here I am, with nothing to wear!*

Wait a minute! What's this? Hannah squeals. On a hanger, way back in the corner, is an outfit her mother has forbidden her to wear. *Mom's already left with the carpool for bratty Jason and Tiffany...so why not?*

This is Hannah's big chance to wear these blacklisted clothes.

If I play this right, I can grab a Pop-Tart and be out the door before good old Dad gets a look at what I'm wearing, Hannah decides. *Everyone at school wears cool clothes like these. A little skin showing is no big deal. I'll blend right in. And there's that new guy...maybe he'll notice me when I'm wearing this outfit.*

Hannah paused, thinking of her mom again. *So what if I get caught? I can always say I didn't have anything else to wear,* she rationalizes.

Mirror, Mirror on the Wall

Dear friend, do you know that what you wear on the outside is a mirror of what's happening (or not happening) on the inside—in your heart and mind? Hannah's made a choice about what she's going to wear to school. Would you have made the same choice?

It may surprise you to know that God cares what you wear. And He wants to be consulted about your choices every day, including your outfit. In fact, He has a lot to say about what we wear. As a Christian, Hannah is God's representative and a walking advertisement for Him.

So what is God's dress code? What are His guidelines? And what does He consider fashion blunders?

Guideline #1—Modesty. Uh oh! This sounds so old-fashioned. But it's something God considers important, so it's a forever concept. The Bible says to "dress modestly" (1 Timothy 2:9). *Modesty* is defined as "a lack of excesses or pretense or show." It describes clothing that is "appropriate" for a young woman who loves God and desires to follow Him. Modesty means avoiding extremes. It means be careful not to wear too much makeup, jewelry, and expensive clothes. Also be careful to wear enough—meaning avoid skimpy, tight, revealing clothes. These are just a few ideas, but I'm sure you get the picture.

Unfortunately, our mainstream culture isn't interested in modesty or moderation. In fact, its motto is the opposite: "Anything goes. Push the limits. Express yourself. Show off your body." God calls us away from such thoughts and standards. He points us to *His* standards.

✎ *From God's Word to Your Heart...*

Romans 12:2 points the way to living life God's way and making the choices He wants us to make. As we go through the verse, jot down your thoughts about how these commands from the Lord apply to you and affect your choices.

"Do not conform any longer to the pattern of this world." Don't let the world squeeze you—a young woman after God's own heart—into its ungodly mold. Don't copy the extreme or edgy customs and fashions of this world.

"Be transformed by the renewing of your mind." Let God remold your mind from within. He'll change your outlook and thinking to match the transformation He is working in you. Turn your back on the world and its ways so you can take on the new ideals and attitudes of Christ.

"Then you will be able to test and approve what God's will is—his good, pleasing and perfect will." In other words, you'll be able "to find and follow God's will; that is, what is good, well-pleasing to Him and perfect."[1]

Here are some good questions to ask when you reach for your clothes: What's my motive for wearing these clothes? Is it to conform to the world's standard—to fit in? Is it to draw attention to me in some way?

God desires His people, regardless of age, to have high moral standards, and that starts with what we wear.

Guideline #2—Decency. First Timothy 2:9 also says to "dress… with decency." We could also use the word *respectable* here. Let me ask you, Who are the most respected kids in your school? Are they the ones who go along with the crowd? Or are they the ones who stand out from—and above—the crowd? The most respected kids are usually admired because they have high standards for their conduct, character, speech, grades, athletics, and commitments.

Do you want to be respectable and respected? I'm sure you do! Then set a high standard for what you wear. And remember, what may be respectable for the world will not always be right for someone who's a Christian. Your love for Jesus is where you'll find the basic standard for your choice of clothes.

Guideline #3—Propriety. God's Word goes on to list another standard for your dress: "dress...[with] propriety" (1 Timothy 2:9). *Propriety* means proper, correct, right. Ask, "What is proper, correct, and right for me as a Christian to wear?" A girl who has a humble heart devoted to God chooses her clothes carefully. She makes sure her choices reflect her position as a daughter of the King, the Lord Jesus. She takes great care not to dishonor the name of Jesus before a watching world.

Guideline #4—Parents. Hannah was given standards to follow by loving parents, but she was choosing to step outside them. When your parents give biblical advice and you listen to them, several things happen. First, you honor God's desire that you respect your parents (Deuteronomy 5:16). Second, you can expect things to go well—or better—for you because God adds a blessing to those who keep His commandments (see the last part of verse 16). And third, you won't be doing foolish things, such as dressing in a revealing way to attract a guy sexually or going to extremes to fit in with the crowd. (Any boy who's interested in you because of suggestive clothing isn't right for you. And anyone who bases friendship on what you wear or don't wear isn't really a friend either.)

What's a Woman to Wear?

How does a woman discern the sometimes fine line between proper dress and dressing to be the center of attention? The answer starts in the intent of the heart. A woman should examine her motives and goals for the way she dresses. Is her intent to show the grace and beauty of womanhood?...Is it to reveal a humble heart devoted to worshiping God? Or is it to call attention to herself and flaunt her wealth and beauty? Or worse, to attempt to lure men sexually? A woman who focuses on worshiping God will consider carefully how she is dressed because her heart will dictate her wardrobe and appearance.[2]

✎ *From God's Word to Your Heart...*

Let's look at some additional principles God gives us to help us choose what to wear and not wear. These guidelines will help you make the right choices—God's choices. You may want to look at each verse in the version or translation of the Bible you usually use. Write down what each verse is saying to your heart.

Develop inner godly character. This is your best outfit! *"She is clothed with strength and dignity; she can laugh at the days to come"* (Proverbs 31:25).

Don't follow the crowd—you have a higher standard. *"Dear friend, do not imitate what is evil but what is good"* (3 John 11).

Seek God's approval. *"Charm is deceptive, and beauty is fleeting; but a woman who fears the LORD is to be praised"* (Proverbs 31:30).

Be careful what you wear. Your clothing sends a message, so make sure you know what that message is. *"Out came a woman to meet him, dressed like a prostitute and with crafty intent"* (Proverbs 7:10-11).

Wear what is right for the occasion. Remember, you are the daughter of the King. Paul taught, *"I also want women to dress modestly, with decency and propriety...with good deeds, appropriate for women who profess to worship God"* (1 Timothy 2:9-10).

Your Heart Response

Think about it. Clothing choice happens daily. Every morning you're confronted with a heart issue: Will you put God at the center of your life in a way as simple and practical as what you wear? Will you seek to please Him? Will you thoughtfully and prayerfully choose clothing that honors God and speaks well of Him? Will you choose to wear what is appropriate for people who profess to worship God?

Make it the desire of your heart to dress to impress God. Dress to catch the look of approval in His eyes. Dress to draw attention to your Savior, your godliness, and your good works so that God is honored (Matthew 5:16). Choosing what you wear is not a small thing. No, it's a biggie! So send the right message.

What or who are your guidelines? First, know what the Bible says. The verses shared in this chapter are a good guide. Also pray. Ask God what He wants...and make the commitment to please Him. Your youth leader or his wife, an older Christian teen you admire, or a Christian college woman you respect are good resources. Ask their opinion. And yes, your mom is a great person to check with too. Then choose carefully and prayerfully what you'll wear. You can make a powerful statement by dressing in a fresh, pure, innocent style. Yes, you can wear clothes that are cute, fashionable, clean, neat, and still follow God's guidelines. If you concentrate on what will be pleasing to God, on following Him and His Word, you should be just fine.

~~~ *Girls Helping Girls* ~~~

❈ Jot down three evidences that Hannah was not giving her clothing choices the proper attention.

-
-
-

❈ What would you tell Hannah about making better clothing choices?

❈ Of the verses shared in this chapter, which one meant the most to you and why? How would you pass that on to Hannah?

❈ In what ways are you like Hannah? If you need to, what new choices will you start making about your wardrobe?

"I Have Nothing to Wear!"

Having "nothing to wear" isn't new. In fact, "I have nothing to wear" is a line from *Sense and Sensibility,* published by Jane Austen in 1811. King Solomon wrote, "There is nothing new under the sun" (Ecclesiastes 1:9), and that's certainly true!

Want to Know More? Check It Out!

✓ True beauty is a matter of the heart. Read 1 Peter 3:3-4. What standards are set, and what strikes you most?

✓ Respond to these phrases in 1 Peter 3:4. (You can use the phrases found in your favorite version of the Bible.) What do you think they mean, and how do they apply to you?

- the "inner self" or the "hidden person of the heart" (NIV and NASB)

- "unfading beauty" (NIV)

- a "gentle and quiet spirit"

- of "great worth in God's sight"

✓ When it comes to your outward appearance, how does 1 Samuel 16:7 influence your thinking?

-

-

God's Guidelines for Making Right Choices

❀ *Develop godly character.* "She is clothed with strength and dignity; she can laugh at the days to come" (Proverbs 31:25).

❀ *Seek God's approval rather than that of the world.* "Charm is deceptive, and beauty is fleeting; but a woman who fears the LORD is to be praised" (Proverbs 31:30).

❀ *Watch what you wear. Your clothes send a message.* "Out came a woman to meet him, dressed like a prostitute and with crafty intent" (Proverbs 7:10).

❀ *Wear what is appropriate for the occasion and for a daughter of the King of kings.* "I also want women to dress modestly, with decency and propriety...with good deeds, appropriate for women who profess to worship God" (1 Timothy 2:9-10).

❀ *Don't worry about following the crowd. You have a higher standard—God's!* "Dear friend, do not imitate what is evil but what is good. Anyone who does what is good is from God. Anyone who does what is evil has not seen God" (3 John 11).

Choice 6

What's That in Your Mouth?

Daniel resolved not to defile himself with the royal food and wine.

DANIEL 1:8

*H*annah glanced out her bedroom window and noticed that the day looked on the cool side. *Perfect! My light coat will cover my clothes until I get to school.* She puts it on and bounds down the steps into the kitchen (wearing the "forbidden" clothing underneath, of course). Everyone has left the house except her dad, who's buried in the morning newspaper and having his last cup of coffee before he leaves for work. Hannah is counting heavily on her dad's normal routine of hardly ever looking up. She moves to the cupboard, her back to him, and says in her most cheerful voice, "Hi, Dad! I'm running a little late, so I'll just grab a Pop-Tart. I don't want to miss the bus. Looks like someone fixed a really good breakfast for everyone. See you later!" She quickly turns and dashes out the door.

Obviously a Pop-Tart isn't going to satisfy Hannah's hunger and need for energy for long. She's already thinking about what she can get from the vending machines at school. Then she winces as she recalls the rumor that the school board is considering banning candy and snack machines in the schools. Hannah hope, hope, hopes this won't happen. Why, she and her friends would starve to death!

You Are What You Eat

Have you ever heard "you are what you eat" before? Some people might debate this statement, but from my own experience I know it's true. I remember all too well when I desperately tried to get the energy I needed from the wrong foods. I drank Cokes galore and consumed candy bars and potato chips all day. And there were the cookies I devoured...especially the cookie dough! These food choices were good for a quick fix as I bustled about being a young wife and the mother of two preschool daughters. But within a short time I was slumped in a chair, a deep fog in my brain, wondering, *What's wrong with me? Why don't I have any energy?*

Finally I went to the doctor, thinking I had mono or was anemic or something. To my surprise, the diagnosis was "too much sugar." My body couldn't process all the sugar it was getting. No wonder I was tired, sluggish, drowsy, and needed a nap every day after lunch. I was a junk food addict, and I was suffering from the "sugar blues."

Better Eating God's Way

Does it surprise you that God has a lot to say about food? In His Word He's very specific. In Old Testament times God restricted what His people could eat. (You can read about these restrictions in the book of Leviticus.) Why did the God of the universe take the time to give His people a detailed set of rules for eating?

First, there were medical reasons. People in those days had no concept of how diseases started or were transferred, so they ate anything and everything, sometimes without even cooking it. By following God's strict rules, the Israelites were healthier and more productive.

Second, by following God's rules for eating, the children of Israel were set apart from those who didn't know or follow God. They were "different." Their food restrictions kept them from mingling with and being caught up in the cultures around them that worshiped false gods.

Third, even these many thousands of years later, life and living haven't changed in some ways. Scientists and doctors are discovering what God knew and passed on to His people so long ago: Not all foods are good for us. Also, the way food is processed and cooked is key to good health and high energy.

✎ *From God's Word to Your Heart...*

In the Bible we learn about Daniel, a teen like you. When the nation of Israel was taken in battle, Daniel was forced to go to a foreign land as a slave. He would have to live and act according to different standards—even in the area of food. Track the choices he made as you read these scriptures. Note what you'd do or how you'd feel if you were in Daniel's sandals.

Daniel's dilemma—"The king assigned [Daniel and other young men] a daily amount of food and wine from the king's table" (Daniel 1:5). Remember, this is in a foreign land, so the food and its preparation wouldn't conform to God's rules.

Daniel's determination—"Daniel resolved not to defile himself with the royal food and wine, and he asked the chief official for permission not to defile himself this way" (verse 8). Do you think it was dangerous for Daniel, a captive, to question what was put in front of him and to refuse to eat it? Also, how's your resolve?

Daniel's declaration—"Daniel then said to the guard...'Please test [us] for ten days: Give us nothing but vegetables to eat and water to drink. Then compare our appearance with that of the young men who eat the royal food'...At the end of the ten days [Daniel and his friends] looked healthier and better nourished than any of the young men who ate the royal food. So the guard took away their choice food and the wine they were to drink and gave them vegetables instead" (verses 11-14). Note the alternative Daniel presented to solve his dilemma and the results.

The king's decision—"At the end of the time set by the king to bring them in...the king talked with them, and he found none equal to Daniel, Hananiah, Mischael and Azariah; so they entered the king's service" (verses 18-19). Note how God honored Daniel and his friends' choices.

Eat to Glorify God

Are you wondering, *Do you mean I can honor and glorify God even when it comes to what I eat?* The answer is *yes*. That's exactly what happened with Daniel and his three friends. They chose to watch what they ate, and God and His standards were honored. And in the end God blessed these four teens. Verse 17 says, "To these four young men God gave knowledge and understanding of all kinds of literature and learning. And Daniel could understand visions and dreams of all kinds." And verse 20 states, "In every matter of wisdom and understanding about which the king questioned them, he found them ten times better than all the magicians and enchanters in his whole kingdom."

Moving to the New Testament, another scripture that emphasizes eating as a spiritual process is 1 Corinthians 10:31: "Whether you eat or drink or whatever you do, do it all for the glory of God." Yes, it's possible for us to eat in a way that honors and exalts the Lord. We give glory to God in an everyday way when we choose to follow His rules for better eating, which leads to better living…God's way.

Rule #1—Eat the right food. Eat healthfully. That's the choice Daniel and his friends made. They chose to eat what produced the greatest health, strength, energy, and stamina. It doesn't take a degree in science or nutrition to know that a Pop-Tart for breakfast isn't the best choice. Or that snacks from the vending machine aren't usually very nutritious. In Hannah's case, her bad food choices were set in motion by getting up late and missing out on the breakfast prepared by her parents. (Yep, more wrong choices that can be traced back to failing to get up on time.)

Choosing to eat regularly and to eat the right foods has two main benefits. The first is *physical*. You'll feel better. (Trust me—I know firsthand the difference right eating makes.) The second is *financial*. How much does junk food cost? Hannah spent most of her allowance on junk food, which left little or no money for more important things, such as giving at church, saving for personal items, or giving gifts. (Come to think of it, Hannah still owes her friend Maria $5 for the snacks she "needed" after she ran out of allowance last week.)

Eating right will give you the strength and energy to fulfill God's plans for your day, and it'll keep your money in your pocket. A win–win situation!

Rule #2—Eat what is sufficient. Overeating is a big problem today. We generally have so much money and food that it's easy to fall into bad habits in the area of eating. But no matter how much we have, God says to eat only what is sufficient, what is needed, what is enough (Proverbs 30:8). In other words, don't eat too much. Why? It doesn't glorify God when we lack self-control. The Bible calls a person who eats too much a "glutton" and condemns his or her actions the same way it does drinking too much. Both cause people to "come to poverty" (Proverbs 23:21).

Making Better Food Choices

Every day is a golden opportunity to make better choices. Every morning can become a time of determining to turn away from bad habits and embrace healthy alternatives. You can make a decision that is truly life-changing today. If food choices are a problem for you, consider taking these steps…today.

Step 1—Realize your body belongs to God. "Do you not know that your body is a temple of the Holy Spirit, who is in you, whom you have received from God? You are not your own; you were bought at a price. Therefore honor God with your body" (1 Corinthians 6:19-20).

Step 2—Recognize that overeating is a sin just like getting angry, stealing, or telling a lie.

Step 3—Recognize if overeating is a problem for you. (A problem defined is half-solved.)

Step 4—Realize you can ask for God's help. Overeating is a spiritual issue as well as a physical problem. God is willing and able to help.

Step 5—Recruit the help of others. Ask friends or an adult you respect to hold you accountable for making better choices concerning food. For starters, try talking this subject over with your mom. No one loves you more than your mom and dad. And your mom probably plays a huge role when it comes to the food purchased, put in the kitchen, and served at home.

Step 6—Eating involves personal choices. No one holds a gun to your head when it comes to eating. Follow these choices daily. Each one of them is under your control:

- Eat only when you're hungry.
- Eat only after you pray.
- Eat only one helping.
- Eat half-portions.

- Eat on a small plate.
- Eat on a schedule that's normal and gives you real energy.

Step 7—Realize if you don't eat enough. Many teens (and adults too!) don't eat enough. Some are literally starving themselves to death. To serve God, to do what He wants you to do, and to help others requires good health and energy. Good nutrition in the right amount gives you health, vitality, and stamina for handling the demands of each day. It also gives you physical stability and mental balance that enable you to manage emotions and think straight when crises come your way.

Your Heart Response

Eating right—eating the best, most nutritious foods in the correct amounts—is a battle. And it's hard for me too. Most of us constantly fight "the battle of the bulge." What to eat and not eat is a necessary choice we make many times each day. We're faced constantly, probably hourly, if not minute by minute, with having to choose when, where, what, and how much to eat. Yet God calls us to a lifestyle of self-control (Galatians 5:23), moderation (1 Timothy 2:9), and wisdom (Colossians 4:5), even in the area of the food we put into our mouths. Do you want to honor

God, excel for Him, and help others? I know you do! Ask Him to help you make the right choices when it comes to food.

~~~~ *Girls Helping Girls* ~~~~

❀ Jot down several bad choices Hannah made in the area of food.

❀ What would you tell Hannah to do differently tomorrow?

❀ Of the verses shared in this chapter, which one meant the most to you and why? How would you share that principle with Hannah?

❀ In what ways are you like Hannah? If you need to make new choices, what are they? What will you do first?

Want to Know More?
Check It Out!

✓ Here are a few more verses and principles about what we put into our mouths. Write out the scriptures and note how each one applies to you and your choices.

Romans 14:17—

1 Corinthians 6:19-20—

1 Corinthians 10:23—

1 Corinthians 10:31—

Galatians 5:23—

God's Guidelines for Making Right Choices

❃ *Do everything to the glory of God, including what you eat.* "So whether you eat or drink or whatever you do, do it all for the glory of God" (1 Corinthians 10:31).

❃ *Bite by bite, give God control of your food intake and appetite.* "The fruit of the Spirit is…self-control" (Galatians 5:22-23).

❃ *Eat only what improves your life.* "'Everything is permissible for me'—but not everything is beneficial. 'Everything is permissible for me'—but I will not be mastered by anything" (1 Corinthians 6:12).

❃ *Don't let inactivity rob your strength.* "The sluggard buries his hand in the dish; he will not even bring it back to his mouth!" (Proverbs 19:24).

❃ *Look to Christ for help to avoid overeating or undereating.* "Clothe yourselves with the Lord Jesus Christ, and do not think about how to gratify the desires of the sinful nature" (Romans 13:14).

Choice 7

What's That Coming Out of Your Mouth?

*May the words of my mouth
and the meditation of my heart
be pleasing in your sight, O LORD.*

PSALM 19:14

Finally Hannah is out of the house—late and racing to the bus stop. She's sprinted this trek many times, and today is no exception. At last she leaps onto the bottom step and into the bus just as its doors are closing. "Whew, made it again!" She waves her student pass to the annoyed driver, who endures Hannah's exploits on a daily basis.

Hannah walks back to where her school buddies always sit. "Hey!" she says, and plops down in the midst of the girls who barely respond to her greeting. Why? Because they're intently involved in learning and sharing the latest gossip. *Oh, yum!* Hannah thinks as she heartily joins the discussion. She's definitely in her element!

"Did you hear…" starts one girl as she shares the latest. Then another girl cuts in, "But I heard it differently." Quickly Hannah throws her two cents of information into the gossip mill, and together the group grinds away on anyone and everyone's activities, clothing choices, reputations, and achievements. Nothing and no one is off limits, whether it's the good, the bad, and... especially...the ugly.

The Truth About Gossip

The word *gossip* doesn't sound so awful, does it? I looked it up in my dictionary, and it describes gossip as a "casual conversation about other people." That doesn't sound so bad either. But what about another word? What comes to your mind when you hear *slander?* A slanderer is "one who makes a false or damaging statement about another person's reputation." Now that's a totally different issue. And yet, slander and gossip can be so closely related that it's difficult to tell them apart.

The Bible contains a list of qualities that are admirable in Christian women of all ages. In Titus 2, verses 3 and 4, we read that older women are to use what they know to "train the younger women." One of those life lessons is "not to be slanderers." This means gossip and slander are *not* godly qualities and are therefore out—off limits—for you and me because we're Christians. For sure, it's hard not to gossip, but gossip is to have no place or part in our lives.

The word *slanderer* is used many times in the Bible, and it has a frightening meaning. It comes from the Latin word *diabolos,* meaning a malicious gossip or false accuser. The word is used 34 times (yes, 34!) in the New Testament as a title for Satan. It's also used to describe Judas, the disciple who betrayed Jesus and whom Jesus called "a devil" (John 6:70). Besides these references, *slanderer* is used in Titus 2:3 and *malicious talkers* is used in 1 Timothy 3:11 in reference to women, literally meaning "she-devils."

Not very good company, is it? Being lumped together with Satan, Judas, and slanderous "she-devil" women isn't a pretty or pleasant thought. Even Hannah might be ashamed of her gossiping if she realized she was acting as a she-devil involved in slandering others.

✎ *From God's Word to Your Heart...*

Sadly, the Bible shows us many females who participated in the destruction of others through ungodly, unchecked gossip. Mark the verses below as you discover more about gossip and slander. Take notes on what hits you about each woman. What did you learn and how can you apply the principles to your life?

Potiphar's wife—She slandered and falsely accused the righteous Joseph. (Read the details in Genesis 39:7-20.) "Now Joseph was well-built and handsome, and after a while his master's wife...said, 'Come to bed with me!' But he refused...Then she told [her husband a false] story...[and] Joseph's master took him and put him in prison." Bottom line? Potiphar's wife's lies cost Joseph three years in prison.

Jezebel—This influential woman set up a situation that falsely framed the God-fearing Naboth. (Read the details in 1 Kings 21:5-14.) On Jezebel's orders, "two scoundrels came and...brought charges against Naboth before the people, saying, 'Naboth has cursed both God and the king.' So they took [Naboth] outside the city and stoned him to death." Bottom line? The lies resulted in Naboth's death.

Martha—Sadly, Martha maligned both her sister and her Lord. (Read the scenario in Luke 10:38-42.) In one sentence she rails against Jesus, doubting His love and care, and accuses her sister, Mary: "Lord, don't you care that my sister has left me to do the work by myself?" The truth? Mary helped Martha with the work…until Jesus began to teach. And Jesus cares about His followers—all of them!

Aiming for Godly Speech

Obviously "godly speech" goes way beyond just not gossiping. It also includes choosing not to lie, curse, tell dirty jokes, or use sexually suggestive or "filthy language" (Colossians 3:8). But right now we're shining the spotlight on gossip because it can sometimes seem so harmless. Besides, everyone does it.

Gossip *always* has a negative effect. I hope you're as struck by those awful definitions and illustrations I shared as I was. And since you're reading this book, I'm sure you desire to follow God's calling to godly speech. For a long time I failed miserably at not gossiping. But then I learned the truth about it. After that I began to live out God's command to put away all malice and evil speaking (Ephesians 4:31). It hasn't been—and still isn't—easy, but I'm committed to making the effort every day. It's been life-changing!

How about you? Are you ready to aim for godly speech? If so, then ask yourself these questions and consider the alternatives and solutions. On the Personal Notes pages at the end of this book, write down what you do to guard your speech and glorify God.

Question #1—How can I avoid gossiping? Put these tactics to work for you. They work!

❀ *Think the best about others.* Assume the best in the actions of others. Apply the guidelines from Philippians 4:8 to what you hear about others: "Whatever is true, whatever is noble, whatever is right, whatever is pure, whatever is lovely, whatever is admirable—if anything is excellent or praiseworthy—think about such things."

❀ *Talk to your friends about gossiping and make a pact to not gossip.* Share with those closest to you your desire to grow in this area. Ask them to let you know when you slip up.

❀ *Be careful in places that are sure to lead to gossip.* Activities like parties, sleepovers, gatherings in the hall at school or during the lunch hour, and phone conversations are perfect settings for gossip.

❀ *Avoid girls who gossip.* There are certain girls who gossip regularly and are skilled at drawing others—including you—into putting down others. Stay away!

❀ *Never name names.* Why? Because anytime you tell a story—even a good one—about someone and use a name, you put yourself in a position for someone else to say, "I heard [your name] talking about so-and-so the other day." And usually the story gets distorted as it's passed on.

❀ *Say nothing.* If your mouth is closed, it's hard to gossip. Have you ever heard the quip, "It's better to be thought a fool than to open your mouth and prove it"? Well, say nothing! You'll be way ahead of the game.

Question #2—How can I work at eliminating gossip from my life? Thinking about these five "T's" will help.

❀ *Time*—Idle time creates opportunities for gossip.

❀ *Tighten up your schedule*—Spend less time hanging out. Always be on your way somewhere—to class, to lunch, to work, to home—so you won't stop and get caught in the web of someone's gossip net.

❀ *Telephone*—Beware of aimless chatting on the phone. When you talk on the phone, preface your calls with a statement such as "I just have a few minutes." Like our friend Hannah, you've already talked to your friends that day, and you'll see them tomorrow and talk again. So limit your phone time. It will keep you out of trouble.

❀ *Talk*—When you do talk, don't talk too long. As

one proverb says, "When words are many, sin is not absent, but he who holds his tongue is wise" (Proverbs 10:19). Be wise and talk less.

✿ *Tarry*—Wait to give input or opinions. You don't have to quickly answer every question you're asked. Sometimes quick answers get you into trouble. Feel free to ask for time to think and pray before (or if) you answer. Proverbs 29:20 says, "Do you see a man who speaks in haste? There is more hope for a fool than for him."

Question #3—How can I make permanent changes in the way I talk? Remember these basic truths and tactics.

✿ *Remember the source of slander*—The devil.

✿ *Realize the cause of slander*—Hatred, jealousy, envy.

✿ *Choose your company carefully*—Pick friends who have only positive things to say about others.

✿ *Choose your activities carefully*—Watch how much you talk on the phone, hang out, or stay in the school lunch area.

✿ *Be generous with praise*—Be known as a girl who's a friend to all. Earn the reputation as one who finds the good in others, who loves others, and who only speaks well of others.

✿ *Pray*—Pray for yourself regarding your speech and also for those who harm you. This way you're telling the right person—God (not everyone else)—about your problems. His job is to deal with those who wrong you (Romans 12:19). Your job is to pray and to forgive.

❀ *Deal with gossip as sin*—Name it for what it is and confess it as sin to God (1 John 1:8-9).

Regrettable Words

I've said some things in my life that I've regretted. One of the biggest things I regret saying involves a girl I barely knew. When I was with a bunch of my friends at a slumber party, I started gossiping about this girl—talking about her behind her back and saying things about her that weren't true. Eventually she found out, and I lost the chance to ever be her friend. I tried to make things right, but she never said another word to me.

It was low of me to try to impress my friends by gossiping about an innocent person. Proverbs 3:29 says that I should not do harm to the people around me. When I gossiped about this girl, I hurt her… and I hurt God too. God created this person in a special way, and when I made fun of her, I was telling God, "That girl or guy isn't good enough for me." And how can we do that when that person is good enough for God?[1]

MEGAN

Your Heart Response

One of the most important choices you make is the choice to monitor your mouth. If you can control your tongue, the Bible says you will be "a perfect [woman], able to keep [your] whole body in check" (James 3:2). What a great goal to aspire to! And, as in everything, the choice is yours. You can slander others… or you can love them.

If you have a heart of love—love for the Lord, love for His Word, love for His people, love for others—then you won't gossip. Gossip and slander pollute your mouth and interfere with what it was created for—glorifying God. I encourage you to start now. Stay true to God's heart. Shine brilliantly as a girl who speaks words of truth and kindness. If you do this, you'll truly be an exceptional woman all the days of your life.

Girls Helping Girls

❀ Jot down several bad choices Hannah made that led to gossiping or being a part of it.

❀ How would you explain the gossip problem to Hannah? What would you tell her to do differently tomorrow? How would you help her?

❀ Of the scriptures shared in this chapter, which one meant the most to you, and why? How would you share this with Hannah?

❀ In what ways are you like Hannah? If you need to make new choices, what will you do first to control what comes out of your mouth?

Want to Know More? Check It Out!

✓ Read James 3:5-12.

How is the tongue described in verses 5-8?

✓ Look up these causes of gossip and answer the questions as you take these sinful "causes" to heart.

An evil heart—What does Luke 6:45 name as a cause of evil speech?

And what does Matthew 15:18-19 name as a cause of evil speech and deeds?

Hatred—To whom (or to what) did David attribute his demise in Psalm 109:3?

Foolishness—Proverbs 10:18 is very direct. What is its message to your heart?

Idleness—What does 1 Timothy 5:13 say about idleness?

How did idleness affect the young women spoken of in this verse?

✓ *Bonus:* What do you learn about gossip from these scriptures?

Proverbs 11:13—

Proverbs 12:18—

Proverbs 16:28—

Proverbs 20:19—

Proverbs 31:26—

Three Categories of Gossip

❊ *Malicious gossip.* Malicious gossip is consciously and deliberately hurtful. It is based in envy and rooted in flagrant selfishness. It is designed to break up relationships and destroy friendships. And it can manifest itself in all kinds of evil deeds.

❊ *Rationalization.* Rationalization is far more subtle than malicious gossip. What makes rationalization so dangerous is that it often results from self-deception. Rooted and based in the same motives as malicious gossip, the person who rationalized has convinced herself that she is doing it for "the good" of the other person. She may disguise it as "prayer interest" and "personal concern." Nevertheless rationalization is very destructive.

❊ *"Innocent" gossip.* This involves a person who truly is concerned, but who is, to a certain extent, unwise and insensitive to other people's feelings. Innocent gossip is sometimes motivated by a desire to be "helpful," but in reality, the gossiper may be trying to prove to others "how helpful she really is." In this situation there is a very fine line between "selfish" and "unselfish" motives. All Christians must be beware of this kind of gossip.[2]

God's Guidelines for Making Right Choices

* *Control your temper.* "Like a city whose walls are broken down is a man who lacks self-control" (Proverbs 25:28).

* *Control your mouth and you will control your life.* "He who guards his mouth and his tongue keeps himself from calamity" (Proverbs 21:23).

* *Commit your mouth to good uses.* "Do not let any unwholesome talk come out of your mouths, but only what is helpful for building others up according to their needs, that it may benefit those who listen" (Ephesians 4:29).

* *Commit your mouth to God.* "May the words of my mouth and the meditation of my heart be pleasing in your sight, O LORD, my Rock and my Redeemer" (Psalm 19:14).

* *Consider that your mouth can do great damage.* "Likewise the tongue is a small part of the body, but it makes great boasts. Consider what a great forest is set on fire by a small spark" (James 3:5).

Choice 8

Choose the Road to Success

*Jesus grew in wisdom and stature,
and in favor with God and men.*

LUKE 2:52

Fortunately, Hannah's gossip session ended abruptly as the bus turned the corner and entered the school campus. Deflated, Hannah realized that the best part of her day had just ended. Now came the dreaded part...*school*.

"Ugh. What a drag. I hate school! And why do I need to go anyway?" Hannah moaned and mourned. "I don't want to go to college, so what's the big deal? And so what if I goof off in class and do average work? It's no biggie."

Hannah went on, dreaming, "If I can just scrape through, do OK, and graduate from high school, everything will be great. I can find a job, get my own apartment, spend my free time hanging out with my friends and doing whatever I like, and have the best time of my life. Who needs school!

"But I guess I've got to endure another school day. Well, there is a bright side! Everyone I hang out with feels the same way."

Somewhat comforted, Hannah entered the school. She sighed. "Misery loves company!" she muttered.

A Dose of Reality

My husband, Jim, often tells the story of how the teens in his childhood hometown struggled with these issues on the importance of school. His town had a major manufacturing plant that hired many of the residents. Every year a large number of high school grads went to work for the tire plant. Most of Jim's friends were counting on these jobs that would keep them in the local area, make life simpler, and provide a fair amount of income. For them, a job at the factory was the road to success.

Like his schoolmates, Jim was headed in the same direction. He was going through the motions at school, not really interested in learning. Then a local pharmacist took an interest in him and hired him. Over the next several years in the pharmacy, Jim turned his focus away from the rubber plant and began to seriously concentrate on his studies so he could become a pharmacist...which he did.

Here's the sad part of the story: The local tire plant closed the year after Jim graduated from college. Many of his high school friends, as well as half the town's population, were suddenly without jobs. And because most of the young people hadn't planned ahead and made some effort in school, their prospects for the future were dashed on the rocks of reality.

✎ *From God's Word to Your Heart...*

God created you and me with minds—minds that are more complex and powerful than any computer. And God expects us to develop our minds. Grab a pen or pencil and look at these verses. Jot down your thoughts about how they can help you develop a better attitude toward learning and school.

> *Listen, my sons [and daughters], to a father's instruction; pay attention and gain understanding* (Proverbs 4:1).

> *Get wisdom, get understanding...Wisdom is supreme; therefore get wisdom. Though it cost all you have, get understanding* (Proverbs 4:5,7).

> *Whatever you do, work at it with all your heart, as working for the Lord, not for [people]* (Colossians 3:23).

Let's look at Jesus' education and knowledge.

> *When he was twelve years old...[Jesus' parents] found him in the temple courts, sitting among the teachers, listening to them and asking them questions. Everyone who heard him was amazed at his understanding and his answers* (Luke 2:42,46-47).

> *Jesus grew in wisdom and stature, and in favor with God and men* (Luke 2:52).

Now write down a brief history of your development, growth, and learning.

The Importance of Today

I'm not encouraging you to spend the next ten years of your life shut up in your room with your head in textbooks. But I'm hoping you're getting the importance of learning what you can every day. Each day of learning is a step on the road to success—the road to positive contributions to society and people's lives, to usefulness, to life options, and to earning and saving money. The good habits and disciplines you develop during the next few years will lay the foundation for the rest of your life. You can choose today—and every day—to grow in your knowledge of the things of God and the knowledge and tools essential for a productive life.

Trust me, you'll never know what the future holds! You don't know what you'll need down the road in the way of education, training, and skills. When I was in high school all I aspired to was teaching office management skills. I loved my classes in that area and wanted to give to others what my teachers gave me. I wasn't a whiz kid or a genius. I struggled to get B's and had to work really hard to get A's. So I wanted to help others who were average like me fall in love with something helpful and fun, something they could use every day to make a living.

Only in time did I use the teaching part of my education… and then it was to teach the Bible! And only in time did I use the typing part of my office skills training…to write books. And only in time did my other office skills help manage our ministry organization. And, my friend, *only in time will you realize God's bigger picture for your abilities and passions,* all to be revealed and grown as you work at being a faithful student.

So why not acknowledge the importance of today? Take advantage of today…and every day…and any and every opportunity to learn and grow. Don't waste these critical years—years that can move you steadily down the road to success. Where are you headed? What do you think the outcome will be?

- ❋ Today's *good decisions* give you the freedom to choose greater opportunities tomorrow.

- ❋ Today's *good habits* give you greater discipline for accepting greater challenges tomorrow.

- ❋ Today's *good attitudes* equip you to run the greater race and win the greater prize tomorrow (1 Corinthians 9:24).

He Died Learning

On the tombstone of a well-known scientist these words were carved: "He died learning." Well, I have to tell you, that message made a staggering impression on me. So much so that I've tried to follow this man's example by becoming a lifelong learner. This attitude has made my life so much more interesting and exciting! I hope you'll make this your motto and goal as well.

Unfortunately, there are teens like our friend Hannah whose motto is "I'd rather die than learn!" They dislike school of any kind (including Sunday school) and can't wait for graduation so they can get on with "real life." Like Hannah, they go through the motions at school and with their homework, exerting only enough effort to get by. Sadly, tomorrow they'll wake up and discover they have very limited job or career options. Why? Because they didn't develop the skills and disciplines needed for the challenges and changes of the future.

"Yeah, I get it. But I'm not a very good student. I try but I never do very well." Is that what you're thinking? Well, there's hope for you! Do you know there are two kinds of learning—formal and informal learning.

Formal learning takes place with textbooks and, in most cases, within the four walls of a classroom, whether at school or at home. Students don't have many options with this type of learning. They learn what the school system dictates or, if you're home-schooled, what your parents require and what the state mandates. Even if it's a struggle, work hard and learn because formal schooling is necessary for life skills and good jobs.

Your efforts at formal learning will give you the foundation and discipline for *informal learning*—for the topics you *choose* to explore outside the classroom. These also give you clues to what you might want to pursue for the rest of your life. Informal study has less to do with ability and more to do with personal interest and desire. The choices are unlimited!

Remember how a pharmacist took an interest in my husband, Jim? Well, informally Jim learned about medical care, medicines, chemistry, and retail sales. The state-licensed pharmacist was a willing teacher, and Jim was an eager student. That informal learning shaped Jim's future—and success—for many years.

You don't need to panic when someone says you have to get an education. There are lots of ways to learn. Look at types of learning this way:

❀ *Learning is an attitude* that involves heart and head.

❀ *Learning is cumulative* and builds upon itself.

❀ *Learning isn't dependent on your IQ*, but on your desire.

❀ *Learning has no boundaries or limits* except those you place on yourself.

❀ *Learning doesn't require social status or money.* It's free to anyone with a desire to expand his or her knowledge.

❀ *Learning has rewards.* The prizes are limitless.

❀ *Learning has an ultimate priority.* You want to know more about Jesus Christ (2 Peter 3:18).

Be a Student for Life

Here are a few *Be's*—simple choices and suggestions—for enjoying the adventures of learning.

Be an eager reader. Reading is the window to learning. It can expose you to the entire globe and to the knowledge and experiences of others on every subject imaginable. Say, for instance, you read one of my books (like this one!). The information you read in a few hours or days took me many years to learn, understand, and put into practice. And it took many more years to discover how to best communicate it to you. In a very short time, you know most of what I know on the subject of making choices. How's that for learning from others?

Caution: You only have so much time. Really! So choose to read books, magazines, and articles that build you up. Read what encourages and inspires you, what teaches and trains you. And don't forget—the first book to read is the Bible. Read it a little at a time. Go from cover to cover or skip around. Just be sure you read it again and again.

Be a person who asks questions. Everyone has something to teach you. Everyone is an expert on something. Find out what that something is and ask questions. Is there someone who's doing something you'd like to do? Ask them about their training. Ask them what you have to do to prepare to do what they do. Asking questions can take a lot of the guesswork out of preparing for your future.

Be a people watcher. Observe the actions of others. Look around you, note what's going on, and copy the good actions of others. Proverbs 20:12 says, "Ears that hear and eyes that see—the Lord has made them both." So pay attention and open your eyes. Who's acting in a responsible way? Who seems to have his or her act together? Who's moving in the direction you want to go? Who has experiences that might give you insights for your own life and future?

Let's say you're interested in missionary work. The next time missionaries visit your church, find an opportunity to ask them about their experiences on the mission field. Or suppose you're interested in photography. Talk to a photographer about his or her experiences. The same goes for any desire—to be a teacher, a jewelry or clothing designer, an architect, a makeup artist... whatever you desire.

And what about the training that God desires for your spiritual growth as outlined for "younger women" in Titus 2:3-5?

Teach the older women to be reverent in the way they live, not to be slanderers or addicted to much wine, but to teach what is good. Then they can train the younger women to love their husbands and children, to be self-controlled and pure, to be busy at home, to be kind, and to be subject to their husbands, so that no one will malign the word of God.

Who are the women in your church who can help you grow in the character qualities listed in those verses?

Another way to learn is by reading autobiographies and biographies of great men and women throughout history. What were their experiences—successes as well as mistakes? If they were Christians, how did they suffer? How was their faith tested? How did they stay true to God? How did they triumph?

And don't forget your Bible! Because the Bible is inspired by God, it is *the best* book for learning and growing.

Your Heart Response

I pray you will never stop learning. Discovering and exploring knowledge develops your most important resource—*you!* And the more you develop *you*, the more God can use *you*. "Whether you eat or drink or whatever you do, do it all for the glory of

God" (1 Corinthians 10:31). To ensure that you're always growing in knowledge, ask yourself these questions every day:

❀ What new thing can I learn today?

❀ Who can I learn from today?

❀ How can I be stretched in some aspect of my life today?

❀ How can I become more Christlike today?

~~~ *Girls Helping Girls* ~~~

❀ Jot down at least three views Hannah has that will limit her choices and hinder her growth in the future.

❀ What would you tell Hannah about the importance of learning in preparation for the future?

❀ Of the verses shared in this chapter, which one meant the most to you and why? How would you pass this information on to Hannah?

❀ In what ways are you like Hannah in regard to school and learning? Do you need to make new choices? If yes, what are they…and when will you start?

Want to Know More? Check It Out!

✓ These people were significantly used by God. Note a common theme in their lives.

Moses was born a slave but grew up to become a great leader of the Israelite people. What contributed to his leadership abilities (Acts 7:22)?

Daniel was a teen when he was carried off to captivity in Babylon. In spite of his situation, he became a man who was greatly used of God. What was part of his preparation (Daniel 1:4)?

How well did Daniel and his three friends prepare themselves (Daniel 1:19-20)?

How much responsibility was Daniel given because of his abilities (Daniel 2:48)?

What influence did Daniel have with the king (Daniel 2:49)?

Paul was a great man who wrote 13 books in the New Testament. Read Acts 22:3. What do you learn about his preparation?

How else was Paul prepared for a life of usefulness, according to Galatians 1:11-12? (Note: Our "revelation" today comes as we read and study God's written revelation, the Bible.)

✓ *You* can contribute mightily to the good of others and in working out God's purposes. But usefulness doesn't come automatically. How should you view preparing for the future?

Do's and Don'ts for Being a Better Student

✿ *Do your homework right away each day.* Do it when you're fresh. You'll feel great and be free once it's done.

✿ *Do your projects in advance.* Don't wait until the last minute. That way if opportunities come up you'll be available, such as a babysitting job, a weekend trip to the beach with a friend and her family, a ball game. Working in advance opens the doors for doing fun stuff without hurting your schoolwork and grades.

✿ *Don't wait until the night before to study for an exam.* Study a while each day in preparation.

✿ *Don't cheat.* It goes against God's Word and His plan for you as a Christian. No grade is worth that.

✿ *Don't be late to school…or to your classes.* In fact, develop the habit of being early. The secret to success in anything is showing up on time or early.

✿ *Don't fail to take notes in class.* Instead of writing notes to others, take notes on the lessons. I once read we retain 10 percent of what we hear, 40 percent of what we read, and 70 percent of what we write down. Note-taking is a shortcut to knowledge.

✿ *Do reward yourself for doing your homework.* Call your best friend…*after* you finish. Turn on your favorite TV program or read another chapter in your exciting book…*after* you finish. Plan to go to the mall with friends…*after* you finish your science project.

❀ *Do keep homework assignments with you at all times.* When you're waiting for a ride, sitting at an orthodontist appointment, or even while commercials are playing during TV programs, you can do some of your homework, make an outline for a paper, go over your notes again for tomorrow's exam, proofread an essay, and so forth.

❀ *Do ask for help.* "The only stupid question is the one you don't ask." If something is missing in your notes, ask your teacher for the information. (Teachers *love* students who want to learn and do better in class.) If you didn't hear part of the teacher's instructions, ask the teacher or another student for the information.

❀ *Don't forget to pray!* You'll be surprised how much difference prayer makes when you do it each morning. Pray that you'll be a better student, pay more attention at school, and be diligent in your school assignments.

A Word About Learning from Socrates

A young man came to the great philosopher and teacher Socrates one day and said, in substance: "Socrates, I have come 1,500 miles to gain wisdom and learning. I want to learn, so I came to you."

Socrates said, "Come, follow me." He led the way to the seashore. They waded out into the water until they were up to their waists. Then Socrates seized his companion and forced his head under the water. In spite of the young man's struggle, Socrates held him under.

Finally, when most of his resistance was gone, Socrates pulled him out on the shore and then returned to the marketplace. When the visitor regained his strength, he went back to Socrates to discover why the teacher had done such a terrible thing.

Socrates said to him, "When you were under the water, what was the one thing you wanted more than anything else?"

"I wanted air."

Then Socrates said, "When you want knowledge and understanding as badly as you wanted air, you won't have to ask anyone to give it to you."[1]

God's Guidelines for Making Right Choices

🌸 *Fix God first in your heart.* "Seek first [God's] kingdom and his righteousness, and all these things [food, drink, clothing] will be given to you as well" (Matthew 6:33).

🌸 *Remember the Lord is the reason for all you do.* "Whatever you do, work at it with all your heart, as working for the Lord, not for men…It is the Lord Christ you are serving" (Colossians 3:23-24).

🌸 *Keep moving.* "She watches over the affairs of her household and does not eat the bread of idleness" (Proverbs 31:27).

🌸 *Focus on what's in front of you, and keep your eye on the goal.* "A discerning man keeps wisdom in view, but a fool's eyes wander to the ends of the earth" (Proverbs 17:24).

🌸 *Give your all to every task, large or small.* "Whatever your hand finds to do, do it with all your might" (Ecclesiastes 9:10).

Choice 9

Make and Keep Friends

Encourage one another and build each other up.

1 Thessalonians 5:11

*H*annah is in the building! The school building, that is. She's slowly making her way through the crowded hall to her locker. She's got to regroup and fortify herself before the start of her first class.

Along the way Hannah meets some of the girls from church. She likes these girls, and they seem to like her too. But there's one problem—these girls aren't very popular. They dress a little differently and act differently too. In fact, Hannah's friend Maria says they're "too nice" and calls them "religious weirdos."

As the church girls turn to go one says, "See ya at youth group tonight!" Hannah gives them all an embarrassed half-smile. She's in turmoil. Why? Because part of her wishes she could be strong and committed to Jesus like these girls are. But she also doesn't want to stand out or be marked as different or weird. Hannah wants to be liked, especially by the "in crowd."

And speaking of the "in crowd," here comes Maria, Hannah's best friend from way back. Maria's beautiful. She wears the latest fashions, and she has a terrific, fun personality. No wonder she's one of the most popular girls in school. Besides that, she always has one or two prominent, great-looking guys from school hanging around. Hannah wishes she could be more like Maria.

Unfortunately, Maria isn't a Christian. And she tries to see how close she can get to the edge...on everything.

Being a Friend

Are you one of those girls who's never met a stranger? You have no problem talking to just about anyone about almost everything. And you make friends easily. Or are you like Hannah, who has a longtime childhood friend like Maria, and the two of you are practically inseparable? For a lot of girls it's not easy to find a good friend. Whether you have many friends or a few, I'm sure you'll agree that friendship is a two-way street. If you want a good friend, you've got to be a good friend.

But what makes a good friend?

✎ *From God's Word to Your Heart...*

Yep! God gives guidelines on how to be a good friend in the Bible. As you read through the following verses, mark what stands out to you. Think of your own friendships and decide if you're trying to be this kind of friend to other girls. And think of what a friend—a real friend—does and doesn't do.

> *He who covers over an offense promotes love, but whoever repeats the matter separates close friends* (Proverbs 17:9).

A friend loves at all times, and a brother [or sister] is born for adversity (Proverbs 17:17).

A man [or woman] of many companions may come to ruin, but there is a friend who sticks closer than a brother (Proverbs 18:24).

Wounds from a friend can be trusted, but an enemy multiplies kisses (Proverbs 27:6).

Do not forsake your friend (Proverbs 27:10).

Being the Right Kind of Friend

How can you choose friends and cultivate friendships that last? As mentioned earlier, developing the right friendships starts with you. *You* need to be the right kind of friend! So what can you do to become a topnotch friend? Take a look at the following choices. If you make them, the best girls will be standing in line to be your friends!

1. *Choose to be growing spiritually.* This is always the first choice to make in every area of your life. And friendships are included. If you desire to grow spiritually and know God more

intimately, you won't settle for anything less than a friend who shares your passion for God. And where do you find girls who love the Lord? Here's a hint: Places where Jesus is talked about. Yes, you'll usually find them at church, in a Christian youth group, or at a Christian camp or activity.

2. *Choose to be yourself.* Don't try to impress others by saying and doing things you think will impress others. And especially don't talk or act in a way that goes against God's Word in any way. Remember, you're looking for a friend who isn't phony, who isn't pretending to be one person when she's really another person. Be who God desires you to be—a godly young woman.

You may or may not be the most popular girl at school, but you will be *you.* You'll be genuine. Authentic. The real thing. And if you're comfortable with who you are—with being a young woman after God's own heart—others will also feel comfortable when they're around you. They might not share your beliefs, but they'll respect you for what you stand for. So be yourself—your wonderful, terrific, super self! God will bring like-minded girls to be your friends.

3. *Choose to be loyal.* Have you heard the phrase "fair-weather friend"? It's a friend who bails as soon as something happens that tests your friendship. She's a great friend…until things get complicated or hard. As long as you do things her way, everything's fine. But the minute you vary from her plans, or try being your own person, or have a real need, or suffer in some way, she fades into the night. She suddenly wants nothing to do with you.

Loyalty is essential in any friendship. So be a loyal friend. You can read about a solid friendship in the Bible, in 1 Samuel 20:14-17. David and Jonathan's relationship was characterized by solid, sincere loyalty. Even in the midst of life-threatening situations, each remained a true forever friend.

How true are you as a friend? Are you "a friend who sticks closer than [a sister]" (Proverbs 18:24)? Loyalty in relationships starts with loyalty in you.

4. *Choose to be honest.* Honesty is another essential in any close relationship. It's one of the benefits and blessings of a true friendship, especially a Christian friendship where you're both living for God and choosing to live according to His principles and rules. You and a best friend should be committed to pulling each other toward God's goals. In fact, you can help each other out by being honest. You can encourage each other in your walks with God.

Remember when I admitted struggling with gossip? Well, I'll never forget tackling that problem. When I learned what God's Word said about gossiping, I knew I needed help. So I told my best friend about my deep desire to make serious changes and, as I put it, "Cut it out!" I asked her to let me know any time I gossiped to her or whenever she heard me gossiping with others. Twenty-five years later that woman is still my best friend. She prayed for me and was honest and let me know when I failed... and helped me over a huge hurdle in my spiritual growth.

As the Bible says, "Wounds from a friend can be trusted" (Proverbs 27:6). It also says to be "speaking the truth in love" (Ephesians 4:15). Your aim is to help one another. You want to be loving and honest so each of you becomes a better person, a better Christian, and a better friend.

5. *Choose to encourage.* Have you thought about how easy it is to tell people all the things you think are wrong in their lives?

A better idea is to get into the habit of noticing the *good* attitudes and actions in others…and letting them know it. You know how terrific it feels to have someone point out something you've done well and praise you for it, so why not do that for others?

What's the best way to be an encourager? Let's go back to David and Jonathan for just a minute. Their relationship was based on their mutual love for God. When David was marked for murder by Jonathan's father, King Saul, "Jonathan went to David…and helped him find strength in God" (1 Samuel 23:16). The Bible says we are to "encourage one another and build each other up" (1 Thessalonians 5:11).

You encourage someone when you help him or her "find strength in God" through the Scriptures and by praying together. Giving sincere compliments also lifts people up. And when you do, be specific. Praise your friends for what you appreciate about them, something you see in their conduct or admire in their character. When you build up people rather than tear them down, you also benefit. Why? Because your friends are a reflection of you. They influence who you are becoming.

6. *Choose to work at friendships.* Good, healthy friendships—the right kind of friendships—don't just happen overnight or even in a week. You have to choose to keep and grow quality friendships. It takes time, care, and effort—a phone call here, an e-mail there, sitting together at lunch, hanging out together. The apostle Paul put it this way to his friends in Philippi: "I have you in my heart" (Philippians 1:7). Do you have a best friend? What can you do today to nurture that friendship?

Finding a Friend

Are you looking for friends? Many girls spend years searching for a friend—a true friend. Take a look around you. While you're making new friends, realize God has already given you quite a few people who will be on your side for years to come.

You have the best friend you'll ever have in Jesus. If you're a Christian, you already have a very special relationship with God's Son, Jesus Christ. He's *chosen you* to be His friend! To His disciples, Jesus said, "You are my friends...I have called you friends" (John 15:14-15). And the same is true for you. And here's a fact: With Jesus as your friend, you're completely and totally loved. He's "a friend who sticks closer than a brother" (Proverbs 18:24). While other friends may come and go or even turn on you, Jesus will be with you, never leaving your side and always encouraging you. You can *always* count on Him. And you can talk to Him through prayer anytime, anywhere, and about everything and anything. Nothing is too trivial or embarrassing or overwhelming.

You have friends in your parents. Before you laugh or tune me out, realize there's nothing weird about having your mom and dad as friends. They are God's gift to you. Hopefully, even if not right now, you'll understand that no humans love you more or want the best for you more than your parents. Ask God to help you develop close friendships with your parents. And be nice to them. Be kind and helpful. Ask for their advice...and then listen with an open heart. In later years you'll be glad you did.

You also have friends in your brothers and sisters. Are you thinking, "Friends with my goofy brother? No way!" or "Friends with my pesky sister? You've got to be kidding!" or "My older sister doesn't want me around." Believe it or not, throughout your life friends come and go. You may stay in touch with some, but most friends you know now will move on. Your family will always be with you, especially if you build and maintain friendships with them. And be encouraged! Your brother won't always be goofy, your sister won't always be a pest, and older brothers and sisters will come to appreciate you.

✎ *From God's Word to Your Heart...*

The Bible is very clear when it speaks to us about the kind of person to look for as a friend...and what kind to avoid. Let's start with God's warnings about who we should avoid. This doesn't mean you aren't going to be kind, friendly, and helpful to everyone. But your close friends—girlfriends and boyfriends—should match God's standards (and yours!). As you read through these verses, make notes about the speech, character, or conduct of those we are to avoid. Also notice the effects wrong friends can have on you.

> *He who walks with the wise grows wise, but a companion of fools suffers harm* (Proverbs 13:20).

> *Do not make friends with a hot-tempered man, do not associate with one easily angered, or you may learn his ways and get yourself ensnared* (Proverbs 22:24-25).

You must not associate with anyone who calls himself a brother [a Christian] but is sexually immoral or greedy, an idolater or slanderer, a drunkard or a swindler. With such a man do not even eat (1 Corinthians 5:11).

Do not be misled: "Bad company corrupts good character" (1 Corinthians 15:33).

Do not be yoked together with unbelievers. For what do righteousness and wickedness have in common? Or what fellowship can light have with darkness?...What does a believer have in common with an unbeliever? (2 Corinthians 6:14-15).

Your Heart Response

There's no question that friendship is an important part of life. And it should be! Friends are a blessing and part of God's love and plan for you. Through your friends God will encourage, teach, train, and grow you into a woman after God's own heart.

As you consider your quest for making and keeping friends, understand there are three kinds of people in life:

❀ those who pull you down

❀ those who pull you along

❀ those who pull you up

Obviously people who pull you down are bad news and should be avoided. The old saying that "bad company corrupts good character" is true. So make sure your friends, close friends, and best friends are Christians who will pull you along and upward toward Christlikeness. They should be strong, like-minded believers who help you think uplifting thoughts, do honorable deeds, and be your finest self.

How do you find such friends?

❀ *Start with yourself.* Nurture the qualities in you that you desire in your friends. Be the kind of person who pulls others along and up toward the things of God.

❀ *Set the highest standards possible* for you and your friends. These standards are what we've been discussing.

❀ *Settle it now.* Decide now that it's better to have no friends at the moment than to have the wrong friends. If you have wrong friends, start looking for friends you can encourage and who will encourage you to Christlikeness.

I've mentioned that Jesus is truly your best and perfect friend. And you can talk to Him about every issue and desire in your heart. Talk to Him often about your friends, your lack of friends, your desire for friends, and any pain you experience from your friends (unfortunately pain is part of life and most close relationships). Jesus understands. He's experienced these things too. And He will encourage you and your friendships, comfort your heart when needed, and give you wisdom. And He will fill any friendship gaps in your life. So talk to Him today!

Girls Helping Girls

✿ Jot down several flaws in Hannah's friendship selection process. What were her standards...what determined who her friends were?

✿ What could you tell Hannah about the importance of carefully choosing her friends? What advice would you give her for making better choices?

✿ Of the verses shared in this chapter, which one meant the most to you, and why? How would you share this with Hannah?

✿ Hannah is in turmoil about who she wants to be friends with. In what ways are you like her? Do you need to make any changes in your life? In your standards? If yes, what are they? What are you going to do first?

Want to Know More?
Check It Out!

✓ Read 1 Samuel 17:57–18:4 (only six verses). Where and when did David and Jonathan first meet?

✓ What words does your Bible use to describe the relationship between David and Jonathan in 1 Samuel 18:1?

What two actions demonstrated Jonathan's deep commitment to his friend David (verses 3 and 4)?

✓ Read 1 Samuel 19:1-2. What was Jonathan's father's plan for David?

What did David's true friend Jonathan do when he found out his father's plan?

✓ Read 1 Samuel 20:17-19, 20-22,36,41-42. Describe the separation that took place between Jonathan and David.

What promise was made by each to the other?

✓ Read 2 Samuel 9:1-7. After Jonathan's death, how did David fulfill his promise he made to his friend?

God's Guidelines for Making Right Choices

❀ *Look for friends who pursue God.* "Flee the evil desires of youth, and pursue righteousness, faith, love and peace, along with those who call on the Lord out of a pure heart" (2 Timothy 2:22).

❀ *Look for friends who are loyal.* "A man of many companions may come to ruin, but there is a friend who sticks closer than a brother" (Proverbs 18:24).

❀ *Look for friends who will hold you accountable.* "Wounds from a friend can be trusted, but an enemy multiplies kisses" (Proverbs 27:6).

❀ *Look for friends who will encourage you toward godly pursuits.* "Carry each other's burdens, and in this way you will fulfill the law of Christ" (Galatians 6:2).

❀ *Look for friends who are like-minded.* "I appeal to you…in the name of our Lord Jesus Christ, that all of you agree with one another so that there may be no divisions among you and that you may be perfectly united in mind and thought" (1 Corinthians 1:10).

❀ *Look for friends who will pray for you.* "Since the day we heard about you, we have not stopped praying for you and asking God to fill you with the knowledge of his will through all spiritual wisdom and understanding" (Colossians 1:9).

Choice 10

Date Without Regrets

Pursue righteousness, faith, love and peace,
along with those who call on the Lord
out of a pure heart.

2 TIMOTHY 2:22

*H*annah's friend Maria has really outdone herself today. As she slinks up to her locker next to Hannah's, she proudly displays her new trendy clothes. In response, Hannah meekly opens her coat and reveals her "forbidden" outfit. She gulps, thinking, *My outfit's way too much for my parents to handle. They'd hit the ceiling if I wore what Maria has on!*

Maria's clothes were very fashionable, but they revealed a lot of skin...more than Hannah was comfortable with. Maria's top was off her shoulders and her tummy showed. She was sure in good shape—and loved showing it off.

The sight of the new clothes was quickly brushed aside as Hannah's eyes met Brad's as he stopped at their lockers. He was a friend of Bill, Maria's boyfriend. He and Bill were great athletes and extremely popular. Just for the record, Brad wasn't technically Hannah's "boyfriend." Yes, they had gone out as part of a group on several occasions, but the relationship hadn't progressed into anything serious…yet. Hannah had high hopes there was more to come. Her parents also liked Brad. They agreed that he was polite, courteous, and well mannered. But they were always pointing out that Brad wasn't a Christian.

Hannah really liked Brad, and he seemed to like her too. So she pushed aside her parents' concern. *Brad's a great guy, so what's the big deal about a difference or absence of religious beliefs?* Besides, Hannah was convinced that if the relationship became serious, true love would transcend any barrier. She also believed that if she and Brad grew closer together, she'd have more opportunities to witness to him about Jesus and maybe influence him so he'd accept Jesus as his Lord and Savior. Then everything would be perfect!

A Word About Boys

In the last chapter we talked about girlfriends and friendships. Now let's look at relationships with boys. You're around guys all day—at school, at church, and in public. How do you act when you're around them? Boy–girl relationships in your teen years are entirely different than girlfriend relationships. I'm sure you're aware of this! So what should be the same and what should be different when it comes to how you are around boys?

With all people you should be friendly and approachable. Treat everyone with respect and consideration. Talk normally and use basic manners. And don't whisper or gossip about people or with them. However, because of the difference between girls and boys and the nature of boy–girl relationships now and in your future, there are some things to be aware of and be careful about. Here are four very important guidelines.

1. *Watch your friendliness level.* Yes, be nice, but maintain a

respectful distance even if the guy is your lab partner at school or participates in an afterschool study group or activity you're involved in. Keep your relationship a bit on the formal side. What does that mean? Be polite. Keep touching to a minimum. Don't spend time alone with him in a private setting. Don't give personal gifts. Getting too close and being too friendly may send the message that you're more interested in him than you are. And if you're interested in him, keep the relationship casual. Don't rush. Although it may not feel like it, you'll have plenty of time for romance in the future.

2. *Watch your compliments.* Don't go overboard on your appreciation or praise. If you like a guy, quietly observe him and his character. Interact with him in a group to see what he's really like. Don't rush or force a boy–girl relationship. If you tell a guy he's cute or awesome, or even tell your girlfriends (who may tell it to someone else...who will tell it to someone else...who will tell it to him), the boy might think you're more interested than you are or you might get more involved than you're ready to. Again, don't try to make a boy–girl relationship happen. And if your relationship is moving in that direction, go slow and be cautious.

3. *Watch how much you talk.* The Bible says you're to have "a gentle and quiet spirit" (1 Peter 3:4). It also says you're not to let unwholesome words come out of your mouth (Ephesians 4:29). This is especially true when it comes to talking with or about boys. If you talk too much, you may say or imply something you're not ready for. If you're a chatterbox, boys may assume you're more interested than you are. They may get the wrong impression about you. (That's easy for boys to do.) Keep

your talk pure. Avoid words with sexual meanings when talking with girls or guys. Boys often view sexual references and words much differently than girls. God wants you to be pure in your body and heart...*and* speech.

4. *Watch what you wear.* God wants you to hold the highest standards for your conduct *and* your choice of clothes. Modesty may sound old-fashioned, but it's His standard, and it will help you steer clear of temptation and potentially harmful situations (1 Timothy 2:9). What you choose to wear has an effect on those around you...especially boys. It's also a sure sign of your priorities—of what's going on in your heart and where you are with God.

When Hannah chose to wear clothes her parents expressly told her not to, she revealed a rebellious spirit toward her parents and, ultimately, toward God. Hannah was looking for approval from the wrong people by drawing attention to herself.

Here's a thought: If wearing revealing clothes is how you get approval from your friends or the boys around you, maybe you need to rethink your friendships. You want to be around people who like you because of your values, your character, and who you are—not because of how your outside looks.

✎ From God's Word to Your Heart...

Boy–girl relationships are certainly exciting to contemplate and be a part of. But please be careful! These relationships can come with a high price tag emotionally and physically. If they're not handled God's way, you may make mistakes or get involved in situations that create lifelong pain and scars. The best way to avoid painful emotions, bad experiences, and regrets is to set high standards—God's standards as presented in the Bible—for your behavior and for the type of guys you consider as boyfriend possibilities. You need a measuring stick, and God has the perfect one for you right in His Word.

The book of Ruth offers great guidelines for what to look for in a potential romantic relationship (if marriage is God's will for you). Look at the qualities highlighted in Boaz, the man Ruth is interested in:

- ❀ *Godly*. Look for a guy with a passion for Jesus. This should be #1 on your list. Boaz asked God through prayer to bless Ruth (2:12).

- ❀ *Diligent*. Look for a guy who's a hard worker. Boaz was a careful manager of his property and wealth (2:1).

- ❀ *Friendly*. Look for a guy who will be your best friend. Boaz gave a warm greeting and welcomed Ruth to his field (2:4,8).

- ❀ *Merciful*. Look for a guy with compassion for others. Boaz asked about Ruth's situation and acted on her behalf and in her best interest (2:7).

- ❀ *Encouraging*. Look for a guy who contributes positively to your growth (in spiritual matters, character development, educational and personal interests). Boaz pointed out Ruth's strong qualities and spoke of them to encourage her (2:12).

- ❀ *Generous*. Look for a guy with a giving heart. Ruth needed food and worked hard for it. Boaz saw that, appreciated it, and arranged for her to be given extra food (2:15).

❁ *Kind.* Look for a guy with a kind heart. Boaz obviously cared for Ruth's well-being. He also cared for Ruth's mother-in-law, Naomi. Naomi thanked God for Boaz's kindness toward her and Ruth (2:20).

❁ *Discreet.* Look for a guy who will protect your reputation. Ruth went to see Boaz in the evening, and he honored her purity and sent her home from the threshing floor before daylight (3:14).

❁ *Faithful.* Look for a guy who keeps his word. Boaz followed through on his promise to marry Ruth (4:1).[1]

Choosing a Godly Approach to Dating

Boaz sounds like a great guy, doesn't he? Do you know anyone like him? If not, be patient. Boys like that are definitely out there! If it's God's will that you be married, He's preparing someone for you right now. In the meantime, there are choices *you* can make as God prepares *you* for the right guy—the best guy.

Choose to associate with boys who are active, vibrant, for-real Christians. Develop—and write down!—a list of character qualities from the Bible that are a must for Christian guys you would be willing to date. Use that list as your guideline for the boys you're interested in and associate with today.

We've looked at Boaz and his godly traits. Check out 1 Timothy 3 and Titus 1 too. God praises men who are blameless in character and pure in conduct. That's the kind of person you want to look for. God desires the best for you, and you should desire the best for you too. Don't settle for less.

Also, never date a guy who is not a Christian. Does this sound harsh? The Bible is crystal clear on this. Second Corinthians 6:14 says, "Do not be yoked together with unbelievers. For what do righteousness and wickedness have in common? Or what fellowship can light have with darkness?" Here's some very wise advice:

> "*Don't buy the 'I can witness to him' myth.* More often than not, when couples relate at different levels spiritually, the Christian is pulled away from God rather than the other way around." The writer goes on to point out how a dating relationship with a non-Christian can only diminish who you are in Christ. There is no way dating an unbeliever can help your walk with Jesus grow stronger.[2]

Choose to focus on group activities rather than on being alone with an individual guy. Use group activities (preferably church activities or get-togethers with Christians) to observe the behavior of the guys in your group. Being part of a group also lessens the temptations that can come up when you're alone with a boy. Another benefit of group activities is the experience you gain in learning to talk to and be with boys. Have fun as you get to know the other kids in the group. There's no pressure in that.

Choose to wait to date seriously until there's a godly purpose or reason—which is marriage. Intense dating at this time in your life can take you on an emotional roller coaster ride that hurts deeply when it ends, or ruins your reputation, or contributes negatively to your character development, or gets you into sexual trouble and scars you for life.

Choose to work with your parents regarding dating. This is a huge sign of maturity. God has made your parents responsible for you. They are accountable to God for everything that involves you. It may be hard to believe, but your parents have experience in dating. They know what goes on between girls and boys in the teen years. Here's a mini-list of ways you and your parents can work as a team when it comes to dating, whether in a group or with an individual. This list will help safeguard you from misunderstandings and painful mistakes.

- ❀ Be sure you ask for and respect a curfew.
- ❀ Be clear about where you can and can't go and who you can and can't spend time with.
- ❀ Be sure your parents meet every one of your friends—girls and boys.
- ❀ Be sure your parents approve of who you're with, where you're going, what you're going to do, and what you're wearing.
- ❀ Be totally honest with your parents.

Choose to remain morally and sexually pure. If you haven't started dating, make this commitment to purity now. If you've already started dating, reaffirm your commitment to God's standard of purity. And remind yourself of your commitment to God's standards *before* every date. This is a spiritual choice… and a wise choice…and a right choice. You're choosing whether you're going to follow Jesus or the world. And here's a heads-up: If a guy tempts you into any kind of activity or action that goes against God's standards or your parents' boundaries or entices you into something that may lead to something against God's standards, he is absolutely *not* the guy for you. He's out! If a boy loves Jesus and truly cares about you, he will desire sexual purity for himself and for you. And he'll be encouraging your spiritual best, not tempting you to moral failure.

Your Heart Response

Who and when you date are very important choices. Please don't approach dating casually. And please don't jump into it just because everyone else is dating. This area is very difficult for Christian girls—and boys. In books, ads, magazines, and on TV dating—and so much more—is portrayed as normal and popular. But if you look beyond the glamour and read stories based on real-life, you'll discover that relationships and dating are difficult areas. You'll see how very easy it is to make wrong choices that will hurt you and others.

So what can you do while you're waiting to date? Like I've suggested, make a list of the godly qualities to look for in those you date. It's so easy to confuse *cute* with *character*, so be careful.

Be patient as you wait to date. Character—yours and the people's you date—takes time...even years...to fully develop. Pursue godliness in your own life and trust God to bring the right boy to you.

And above all, enjoy being you. Enjoy your life now. Make good girlfriends. Spend your time—and emotions—on people and activities at home, at church, at school. Be careful not to obsess on a guy (or guys). God wants your mind on Him—on growing spiritually, on living His way, on developing into the woman He created you to be. You are first and foremost a young woman after His own heart.

Girls Helping Girls

❀ Jot down three wrong assumptions and wrong approaches Hannah had about guys and dating.

❀ What would you tell Hannah to help her understand the seriousness of making right choices about boys and dating?

❀ Of the verses shared in this chapter, which one meant the most to you, and why? How would you pass that on to Hannah?

❀ In what ways are you like Hannah? Are there choices you need to make regarding boys to better align with God's standards? If so, what will you do first?

Want to Know More?
Check It Out!

✓ What does 2 Corinthians 6:14 say is *the* most important choice you need to make regarding boyfriends and dating?

✓ What do these verses say about how boys should treat you?

　　1 Corinthians 13:4-7—

　　1 Peter 2:17—

　　Ephesians 4:32—

✓ What do these verses say about what the best attitude and behavior are when it comes to you and boys?

　　1 Samuel 16:7—

　　Matthew 5:8—

　　1 Thessalonians 4:4—

　　1 Peter 3:3-4—

The Best Time

Recently this boy asked me to be his girlfriend. I told him no because I think I'm too young to get into that kind of thing. And my mom doesn't want me to date until I'm sixteen anyway. I knew it just wasn't the right time.

It's important to realize that love isn't something to play around with. Song of Songs makes that clear when it says, "Do not arouse or awaken love until it so desires" (Song of Songs 2:7). We shouldn't run into a dating relationship simply because everyone else thinks it's OK. God wants us to wait for the right person, not because he doesn't want us to have a good time but because he wants us to have the *best* time.

Because God cares about us so deeply, he wants us to save romantic love for a relationship he would be proud of. We don't know when or if that will happen, but we can trust God to take care of us in his way and in his time.[3]

ROBYN

God's Guidelines for Making Right Choices

❀ *Don't date unbelievers.* "Do not be yoked together with unbelievers...what fellowship can light have with darkness?" (2 Corinthians 6:14).

❀ *Realize an unbeliever doesn't have God's best in mind.* "Those who live according to the sinful nature have their minds set on what that nature desires" (Romans 8:5).

❀ *Look for godly actions in others.* "Love is patient, love is kind. It does not envy, it does not boast, it is not proud. It is not rude, it is not self-seeking, it is not easily angered, it keeps no record of wrongs...It always protects, always trusts, always hopes, always perseveres" (1 Corinthians 13:4-7).

❀ *Look for godly character.* "Do not consider his appearance...Man looks at the outward appearance, but the LORD looks at the heart" (1 Samuel 16:7).

❀ *Don't settle for less.* "If anything is excellent or praiseworthy—think about such things" (Philippians 4:8).

❀ *Prepare yourself spiritually.* "Your beauty should [be]...a gentle and quiet spirit" (1 Peter 3:3-4).

Why's a Nice Girl Doing That?

Each of you should learn
to control his own body in a way
that is holy and honorable.

1 Thessalonians 4:4

The bell for the start of first period is already ringing as Hannah and Maria dash down the hall to their history class. As they near the door to the classroom, Maria whispers, "Well...are you in or out?" Before Hannah can say anything, Maria flings open the door and the two enter the classroom... only slightly late this time.

Hannah takes her seat and immediately starts stressing about Maria's question. She knows exactly what her friend is asking, which is why she's so worked up. For weeks Maria and her boyfriend, Bill, have been making plans for a very special date. They're going to tell everyone they're going to the movies Saturday night. What they're really planning to do is go to Bill's house. And Bill's parents are going to be out of town.

Bill and Maria's relationship has intensified physically over the months of their dating. And since Maria loves to live on the edge, Hannah can only imagine what's going to happen at Bill's house. But now, to make matters worse, Maria and Bill want Hannah and Brad to join them to make their alibi look more authentic.

What should I do? Hannah worried. *Maria is my best friend. I don't want to disappoint her. Brad is a great guy, and I really like him. It would be fun to spend time with him. But I've never done anything like this before, and what would my parents say if they find out the truth—that we went to Bill's and his parents were gone? And I'm not sure I'm comfortable with what might go on between Maria and Bill. And how would Brad react to that?*

While she's chewing on this giant "crossroad question," the teacher, Mrs. Henderson, hands Hannah the weekly history exam.

Now Hannah faces a more immediate choice: Will she sneak a peek at the answers she's put on a small piece of paper in her sweater sleeve?

The Truth About Temptation

Living the Christian life is a struggle. Jesus said to His disciples—and us—that "in this world you will have trouble" (John 16:33). Some of the trouble Jesus was talking about will come in the form of temptation. When you give in to temptation, that's when sin occurs (Matthew 5:28). That's why you have to fight temptation. You don't want to fall and fail!

One key problem with temptation is that it comes in so many varieties. The target is always your "purity"—ethical purity, mental purity, spiritual purity, and physical and sexual purity. As you can see, Hannah has two temptations going on: lying about the date night and cheating on her history test.

When temptation strikes, remember God expects you to actively "flee the evil desires of youth, and pursue righteousness, faith, love and peace...out of a pure heart" (2 Timothy 2:22).

✎ *From God's Word to Your Heart...*

Think about the following truths, each of them given to you by God. In fact, why not do more than just think about them? Grab a pen and dissect them—take them apart. The more you get out of these verses, the more they'll guide you when you encounter temptation.

> *His divine power has given us everything we need for life and godliness* (2 Peter 1:3).

> *Live by the Spirit, and you will not gratify the desires of the sinful nature* (Galatians 5:16).

> *The acts of the sinful nature are obvious: sexual immorality, impurity and debauchery...But the fruit of the Spirit is...self-control* (Galatians 5:19,22-23).

No temptation has seized you except what is common to man. And God is faithful; he will not let you be tempted beyond what you can bear. But when you are tempted, he will also provide a way out so that you can stand up under it (1 Corinthians 10:13).

Be strong in the Lord and in his mighty power (Ephesians 6:10).

Learning More About Temptation

God has entrusted you with a most important treasure—your purity. And with His help, you can preserve it in every area of your life. As you know, temptations come in a variety of forms and on many levels. The classic example of temptation is Satan's enticement of Eve in the Garden of Eden. It begins with a specific command God gave to Adam in Genesis 2:16: "You are free to eat from any tree in the garden; but you *must not eat* from the tree of the knowledge of good and evil, for when you eat of it you will surely die."

Sometime later, Satan—"the serpent"—came up to Eve to "discuss" and "talk over" what God said to Adam. Eve's chat with the devil went like this:

Serpent: "Did God really say, 'You must not eat from any tree in the garden'?" (Genesis 3:1).

Eve: "We may eat fruit from the trees in the garden, but God did say, 'You must not eat fruit from the tree that is in the middle of the garden, and you must not touch it, or you will die'" (verses 2-3).

Serpent: "You will not surely die…For God knows that when you eat of it your eyes will be opened, and you will be like God, knowing good and evil" (verses 4-5).

The Fall: When the woman saw that the fruit of the tree was good for food and pleasing to the eye, and also desirable for gaining wisdom, she took some and ate it. She also gave some to her husband, who was with her, and he ate it (Genesis 3:6).

The results: Adam and Eve were banished from the Garden of Eden. As God explained to Adam, "You listened to your wife and ate from the tree about which I commanded you, 'You must not eat of it'" (verse 17). From that moment on, the world—including you and me—suffered the consequences of Adam and Eve's giving in to temptation.

Did you catch the progression of temptation to sin? Adam and Eve were told by God exactly what His will was. You and I too are given God's Word, the Bible, so we can know and understand God's will and commands. He did this so we would have no doubt about what He wants us to do and not do.

The first step down the road of temptation is to doubt something God states in His Word, to question His character, His instructions, His purposes, His love, and His mercy for you. So be on guard! Satan and the world are *very* skilled at planting doubt and trying to shake your faith and trust in God.

Certain Choices Are "No-brainers"

1. Will it be legal? (1 Peter 2:13-15)
2. Will my parents approve? (Ephesians 6:1)
3. Will it cause others to stumble? (1 Corinthians 8:12-13)
4. Will it benefit others? (1 Corinthians 6:12)
5. Will it be habit forming? (1 Corinthians 6:12)
6. Will it cause me to grow? (1 Corinthians 10:23)
7. Will it be a good testimony? (1 Peter 2:12)
8. Will it glorify God? (1 Corinthians 10:31)

The Scope of Your Purity

Purity is at the top of God's list for you as one of His precious young women. The word *pure* in the Bible is translated in different versions as "chaste" or "pure-minded." Look up *pure* in your dictionary and you'll find definitions about being without stain, free from pollution, clean, innocent, and guiltless. Purity is a tall order from God. So no matter what your age, pay careful attention to purity.

When your parents or youth leaders talk about purity, what are they usually referring to? Sexual purity, right? This is an important area because physical purity is very special, and God makes it very clear in His Word that He wants us—young and old—to be pure in body.

But physical purity extends beyond just saying no to sex. Purity includes watching what you put into your body. It includes smoking, drinking alcohol, and taking drugs. Here's something to think about. The laws of our country make smoking and drinking illegal until a certain age. And misusing drugs is illegal regardless of age. There are good reasons for these laws, so we obey them. Why? It's the law.

And I'm pretty sure your parents don't want you smoking, drinking, or taking drugs. They love you and want the best for you. And then there's your health. Medical professionals have revealed many ways smoking, drinking, drugs, and overeating are harmful to your health.

These are all good reasons not to indulge in harmful and illegal substances. But the most important reason to keep yourself healthy and pure is God and your service to Him and His people. Join the apostle Paul in his resolve, "I will not be mastered by anything" (1 Corinthians 6:12).

✎ *From God's Word to Your Heart...*

As you thought about purity, did any of the following verses come to mind? How do they relate to you? What do these look like in your life? Make a few "notes to self."

> *Do you not know that your body is a temple of the Holy Spirit, who is in you, whom you have received from God? You are not your own; you were bought at a price. Therefore honor God with your body* (1 Corinthians 6:19-20).

Do not set foot on the path of the wicked or walk in the way of evil men. Avoid it, do not travel on it; turn from it and go on your way (Proverbs 4:14-15).

Finally, brothers, whatever is...pure...think about such things (Philippians 4:8).

Keep yourself pure (1 Timothy 5:22).

Flee the evil desires of youth, and pursue righteousness (2 Timothy 2:22).

So What's a Girl to Do?

This book is all about choices—your choices to do what is right and pleasing to God. Making right choices protects you from sin, failure, and harm. When you come face-to-face with temptation, there are several choices you can make with full confidence, knowing they are the right ones.

1. *Choose godliness*. The first step in maintaining your purity is to pursue a life of godliness (2 Timothy 2:22). The more you read God's Word, pray, worship with God's people, and be

accountable to others, the more you'll realize what's right and wrong according to God. (Our friend Hannah never got around to reading God's Word and praying about her choices. She also had little or no accountability for her actions. No wonder she's struggling so...and not making the *best* decisions!)

2. *Choose to avoid places and situations where you might be tempted.* Paul told his young friend Timothy to "flee the evil desires of youth" (2 Timothy 2:22). *Move! Avoid temptation!* When temptation comes along, run as hard as you can, as fast as you can in the opposite direction.

3. *Choose to avoid people who might tempt you.* Hanging out with friends who pull you down isn't good. In fact, it can be deadly when it comes to temptation. In Hannah's case, Maria is not a very good influence, is she? God's Word leaves no doubt about what Hannah should do—and you too when difficult situations arise: "If sinners entice you, do not give in to them...do not go along with them, do not set foot on their paths" (Proverbs 1:10,15). Yes, this is hard—and sometimes painful—to put into practice. Living for Christ isn't always easy.

4. *Choose to dress modestly.* Are you wondering, "Why this again?" It's because this is not only for your purity, but also for the purity of others. I'm especially talking about boys. They have eyes, you know. So don't be seductive and flirtatious in your appearance. Your values and reputation are affirmed by what you wear. The Bible says you are to be modest (1 Timothy 2:9).

Your Heart Response

My dear young friend, purity is a lifelong calling. You'll be watching over your purity for years to come. And it's an issue of the heart—your heart. Your behavior is determined by where your heart is set. Two of my favorite verses in the Bible are Colossians 3:1-2. These verses tell us to set our hearts and minds on things above, not on earthly things. Make sure your heart's compass is pointing straight toward God and the purity He desires of you, in you, and for you. Guard your heart and mind and body every day. As you live for God, His standards and values will be reflected in your life of purity in thought, word, and deed.

Girls Helping Girls

❀ What flashing red lights are trying to get Hannah's attention so she can make the right choice about the secret Saturday night date?

❀ What could Hannah have done to avoid the temptation to cheat on the test or lie about her plans for Saturday night?

❀ What advice can you give Hannah about the importance of

living God's standards of honesty and sexual purity? How would you tell her?

❋ Of the verses shared in this chapter, which one meant the most to you, and why? How would you share it with Hannah?

❋ If you were in Hannah's position, what would you do? How would you follow God's principles?

❋ In what ways or areas do you struggle with purity? Are there any choices you need to reconsider? To change? To start making now?

Want to Know More?
Check It Out!

The Bible strongly teaches you to refuse to do anything that would affect your purity and hinder your Christian testimony. How will you apply these verses in your life?

✓ Read 1 Corinthians 6:18-20. What is the command in verse 18, and the reason for it?

What do you learn about your body in verses 19-20?

What is the final command in verse 20, and the reason for it?

✓ Read 1 Thessalonians 4:3-8. What are the three parts of God's will (verses 3-4)?

—

—

—

According to verse 5, how do unbelievers behave?

What is the result of sexual sin (verse 6)?

What is the consequence of sexual sin (verse 6)?

What strong message does God give in verse 6 regarding hurting others?

What's God calling to you in verse 7?

When someone rejects God's calling, who and what are really being rejected?

✓ *Bonus:* Read Genesis 39:7-20. How did an immoral woman tempt the godly Joseph? List the evidences of her impurity, her attempts to cause Joseph to sin, and Joseph's responses.

What price did Joseph pay for remaining pure in body and true to God (verse 20)?

My Prayer for Purity

Lord...

> I give You all the desires of my heart—
>> may You bring them into line
>> with Your perfect will.
>
> I give You my mind—
>> may it be filled with thoughts that
>> can be brought into Your holy presence.
>
> I give You my mouth—
>> may I speak only that which honors You,
>> encourages others,
>> and reveals a pure heart.
>
> I give You my body—
>> may I keep it pure so that it is a holy
>> and honorable vessel fit for Your use.
>
> I give You my friendships with young men—
>> may I set my heart on purity.
>> May You have authority over all my passions.
>
> And I give myself afresh to You.
>> Take my life and let it be
>> ever, always, pure for You.[1]

God's Guidelines for Making Right Choices

✻ *Look to God for the strength you need.* "Those who hope in the LORD will renew their strength. They will soar on wings like eagles; they will run and not grow weary, they will walk and not be faint" (Isaiah 40:31).

✻ *Look to God's Word for the growth and wisdom you need.* "Like newborn babies, crave pure spiritual milk, so that by it you may grow up in your salvation" (1 Peter 2:2).

✻ *Look to God for the control you need.* "The fruit of the Spirit is love, joy, peace, patience, kindness, goodness, faithfulness, gentleness and self-control" (Galatians 5:22-23).

✻ *Look to God for help in being an example.* "Don't let anyone look down on you because you are young, but set an example for the believers in speech, in life, in love, in faith and in purity" (1 Timothy 4:12).

✻ *Look to God for victory.* "Thanks be to God! He gives us the victory through our Lord Jesus Christ" (1 Corinthians 15:57).

Choice 12

Turn Your Life Around

*Trust in the LORD with all your heart and
lean not on your own understanding;
in all your ways acknowledge him,
and he will make your paths straight.*

PROVERBS 3:5-6

Hannah has really—*really*—made wrong choices this past week. Yes, she *chose* to give in to the temptation to cheat on her history test. And then there was last night...Saturday night. (Remember Hannah's quandary about going to Bill's house with Brad?) Hannah chose to lie to her parents.

Maria, Bill, Brad, and Hannah ended up at Bill's house—minus his parents. And sure enough, Bill and Maria vanished to another room, leaving Hannah alone with Brad. Their absence seemed to give Brad the green light to move in on Hannah. After a few minutes of snuggling, and to Hannah's credit, she made a right choice. She recognized the danger to her standards and purity and objected verbally and physically. But that didn't stop Brad. He persisted, telling her it was all right and perfectly natural to want to "get closer." He even implied she was being a prude and acting like a child. In a panic, Hannah pulled away, ran into the bathroom, and locked the door. She pulled out her cell phone and called her dad. It was very hard to do, but she quickly explained the situation and asked him to come and get her.

She was so thankful when her dad showed up!

It's Sunday now, and Hannah's mind is going crazy. *How will I ever face Maria? She probably doesn't want to be my friend anymore. She must think I'm such a baby and hopelessly old-fashioned. I'm sure Brad's told everyone about last night. I'll be laughed at—especially by Brad and Bill and their guy friends.*

I know what I'll do. I'll ask my mom to homeschool me—starting tomorrow. Yes, that's it! Or maybe I can move to Cleveland and live with Aunt Millie. She's great…and I won't have to see anyone at school ever again. And I won't have to live with Mom and Dad's disappointment.

As Hannah gets out of the car and heads into her youth group meeting at church, she feels defeated and dejected. Yes, her parents had been pretty supportive and said they were glad she'd called when she needed help. But they were also upset that she'd lied and put herself in such a bad situation. And Hannah didn't blame them. What was even worse was their disappointment. They didn't scream and shout—and they didn't need to. Their faces revealed the pain that she, their daughter, had violated their trust.

Hannah entered the classroom and sat down. Here she was—at church and surrounded by Christians. She felt so ashamed. So foolish. So embarrassed. And even worse was her dilemma about how to face Jesus. How disappointed He must be about what she'd done! And how could she keep from making other bad decisions? Her sorrow was real and heartfelt.

Then Rick, the youth pastor, got up, faced the class, and began talking.

Proverbs 3:5-6

Hannah had always been on the fringe of her Christian friends' social circle. It was her choice, of course. She always went to youth group—her parents made sure of that. But she seldom paid attention to what was happening there. She lived with one foot in the world and one foot in the Christian culture, but most of her focus was on the world's side.

But today she was dealing with regret, confusion, and pain. Suddenly she felt desperate. She wanted help and answers. She knew in her heart that living for Jesus was the solution. But how could she make the decision to dive headlong and whole-heartedly into Jesus when the world and Maria and her other friends were so fun to be around? It was exciting to live on the edge—most of the time, anyway. Torn, she decided to listen to Pastor Rick. For the first time in a *l-o-n-g* time, she made an effort to hear what he had to say.

"Open your Bibles and turn to Proverbs 3. Let's take a look at verses 5 and 6," Pastor Rick said.

(Hannah made a mental note to bring her Bible to the next meeting. For now she'd just listen.)

Pastor Rick continued. "Okay, verses 5 and 6:

> *Trust in the LORD with all your heart and lean not on your own understanding; in all your ways acknowledge him, and he will make your paths straight.*

"Now, let's look at each verse.

"'*Trust in the Lord with all your heart.*' Do you ever feel like there's no one you can trust? No one who understands what you're facing or feeling when you have an important decision to make? It's awful feeling alone! You don't really feel like talking to your parents about it. Your friends are caught up in their own lives. The weight of the world is on your shoulders. You half-pray, 'If only there was someone I could talk to. Someone I could trust with my problems and decisions...'

"And when your list comes up empty, you decide there isn't anyone who can help you. So you make your choice alone. Sometimes your choice is OK. But sometimes it leads to disaster.

"You know what I'm about to say next, don't you? Yes! There *is* someone you can trust 100% of the time with 100% of the choices you have to make. That someone is Jesus. And He knows 100% of the time what is *best* for you. He knows what you need and what's good or harmful for you. In fact, He's the best resource you have!

"You already know this, I'm sure. But now it's time for you to truly believe it...and live it! In every choice you make, from the small ones to the humongous ones, you need to trust and believe that God can—and will—help you make the right choices. That's where the 'with all your heart' part of verse 5 comes in. Can you do that? It sounds hard, I know. But you will never know God's complete will for you without totally trusting Him.

"Next comes '*Lean not on your own understanding.*' God isn't asking you to give up your ability to think and reason. He gave you those abilities! But He is asking you to discover and listen to the wisdom of His Word, your conscience, and to the prompting of His Spirit, not to mention to wise counsel, and to pay attention to the wise counsel of His Spirit."

Hannah's Problem

This was Hannah's problem. She wanted what she wanted. And she was listening to the wrong people—to everyone *but* God. She was totally excluding God and the positive resources He had given her (like His Word and prayer) to help with the choices she faces. Hannah was leaning on her own understanding.

Take, for instance, her decision on whether to go on the Saturday night date with Brad. If she had reached out for help from God, from her parents, or from wise Christians, they would have guided her to the right choice. If she had only stopped, waited, prayed, listened to God and His people, and trusted in His wisdom, she would have been spared a very painful experience.

Pastor Rick continued. "Verse 6 says, '*In all your ways acknowledge him.*' How do you acknowledge the presence of a friend? You call out his or her name. You wave. You flash a smile and yell hi. You may even give him or her a hug or a slap on the back. Acknowledging God is no different. You know Jesus is your best friend, right? He's always with you right where you are. He never leaves you or turns on you! So make it a point to always acknowledge His presence and seek His advice. The best way to do that is by praying. Bring all your decisions to

Jesus. Ask Him to help with your choices. He will! Every one of them is important to Him. He wants to be part of your life, and He wants you to know that and include Him. So ask for His help and wisdom. Pray with a sincere heart, 'Lord, what do *You* want me to do?'

"The rest of verse six says God '*will make your paths straight.*' What does this mean to us? It means we need to examine our values. We all need to do this often to make sure we're living what we believe. Sure, we can seek the Lord's advice when we're backed in a corner or when we've made some not-so-great choices and are facing the consequences. But it's much better to talk to Him *before* trouble arrives.

"What questions can we ask to help us get real and talk to Jesus? Try these:

❋ What is really important to me…and are these areas important to God?

❋ What are my priorities…or, rather, what should my priorities be?

❋ Have I fully given my heart to Jesus in this matter? Am I living that commitment?

"Putting God at the center of your life will assure His guidance in the choices you have to make. As you can see from verse 6, *your job* is to acknowledge God in everything and seek His will. Once you do that, *His job* is to direct and guide you—to make your paths obvious and straight. He will clear out the roadblocks, remove the hurdles, and enable you to move forward. You'll be making the right choices, which means you'll be enjoying life more and suffering less. Isn't that awesome?"

✎ *From God's Word to Your Heart...*

What is the result of trusting in the Lord with all your heart? Grab your favorite pen and make these truths your own. Underline or highlight your favorite part of each verse. Note its message to you and how its revealed in your life.

> *This is what the* LORD *says: "Stand at the crossroads and look; ask for the ancient paths, ask where the good way is, and walk in it, and you will find rest for your souls"* (Jeremiah 6:16).

> *Seek first his kingdom and his righteousness, and all these things will be given to you as well* (Matthew 6:33).

> *Do not conform any longer to the pattern of this world, but be transformed by the renewing of your mind. Then you will be able to test and approve what God's will is—his good, pleasing and perfect will* (Romans 12:2).

> *Whether you turn to the right or to the left, your ears will hear a voice behind you, saying, "This is the way; walk in it"* (Isaiah 30:21).

If any of you lacks wisdom, he should ask God,
who gives generously to all without finding fault,
and it will be given to him (James 1:5).

Knowing About God's Forgiveness

Hannah had found her answer! A light turned on in her brain and heart. And it was so simple. All she had to do was trust God with every detail of her life, and He would help her make the right choices! (Yes, this is easier said than done, but it's a goal to work toward.)

But there was a problem. Hannah didn't think she was worthy. She didn't feel "clean." She was afraid to approach God. She'd chalked up quite a list of sins this week alone: lying, cheating, gossiping, disobeying her parents, and rebellion.

Hannah sighed and wondered, *How can I make a fresh start? How can I get my life turned around? How can God ever forgive me?*

God answered her. He had Pastor Rick explain.

"Let's look at Ephesians 1:7:

In him we have redemption through his blood, the
forgiveness of sins, in accordance with the riches
of God's grace.

"Paul is talking about Jesus. In Jesus we have redemption. God is 100% holy, and He doesn't put up with sin. But all people are sinful. That's a problem...a huge problem. All people are separated from God because of sin. The bad news is that because of our sin, we deserve punishment and death. Romans 6:23 says that. But the *good news* is that because of Jesus' death on the cross, we are spared! If we accept by faith Jesus' death in our place, we don't experience spiritual death. We are forgiven for our sins! It's like they are gone!

"Do you see how important it is to know Jesus as your Lord and Savior? It's only through Him that you can experience complete forgiveness and be granted eternal life with Him forever. If you want to give your life to Jesus right now, pray this simple prayer from your heart:

> Jesus, I know I'm a sinner. I repent of my sins and turn and follow You. I believe You died for my sins and rose again victorious over the power of sin and death. I accept You as my personal Lord and Savior. Come into my life and help me follow You completely from this day forward. Thank You! Amen.

"If you prayed this prayer just now, come up and see me after class. I'd like to celebrate with you!" Pastor Rick said.

Hannah's Dilemma

Hannah already knew in her heart that Jesus was her Savior. She knew her sins had been forgiven when she committed her life to Him at camp last summer. She already belonged to Jesus. But her problem was with handling the everyday life issues that came up and the ongoing daily temptations and sins.

How can Jesus forgive the awful sins I've committed this past week? Hannah agonized. *I neglected God.*

> *I was lazy and selfish. I was horrible to my family.*
> *I purposefully went against my parents' rules and*
> *wishes. I cheated. I lied. I disobeyed God and my*
> *parents.*

Again God came to the rescue. Pastor Rick had paused for the prayer. Now he continued.

"Okay. Are you wondering if Jesus will cover *all* your sins... even the ones you struggle with every day? Let's turn to 1 John 1:9:

> *If we confess our sins, he is faithful and just and*
> *will forgive us our sins and purify us from all un-*
> *righteousness.*

"Because of the sacrifice of Jesus on the cross, our redemption—our salvation—and forgiveness from our sins is unlimited. If we acknowledge our sin with true sorrow and repentance, we can trust in God's willingness to forgive us throughout our lives. Isn't that astounding?"

Hannah's Deliverance

So Hannah's problem with ongoing, daily sin was solved *by* Jesus and *because* of Jesus.

Pastor Rick continued with another prayer—a prayer of recommitment. Hannah didn't hesitate about praying this time. This prayer was just what she needed!

> Jesus, I know in the past I asked You into my life.
> I thought at that time I was Your child, but my
> life hasn't shown the fruit of my belief. As I hear
> Your call again, I want to make a real commitment
> to You, the Lord and Master of my life. I want to
> know that I am *Your* child—and live like it. Help
> me follow You in every part of my life. Amen.

What freedom! Hannah's burden of failure was lifted! She felt clean. She was clean! She was forgiven for her past sins—and the past week!—and was eager to stop living the way she had been and start *really* living for Jesus.

Accepting God's Forgiveness

My dear reading friend, where are you when it comes to forgiveness? Do you need to start with Pastor Rick's prayer of salvation and ask God for forgiveness through His Son, the Lord Jesus? If so, why not do it now? What a great time to give your heart and your life to Christ. There's no time like right now!

Or are you like Hannah—already a Christian, but one who has strayed away from God? Have you made some mistakes, some bad choices? Are you feeling like Hannah did when she wondered, *How can God forgive me? I've done some things I'm terribly ashamed of?* Well, as you can see, God's forgiveness stretches from Jesus' cross all the way to you! Confess your sin and return to Jesus. Give Him full control of all of you. Start now to let Him run your life. He doesn't make mistakes. In fact, He'll do a perfect job.

Moving On

Isn't God great! He's given you and me the gift of salvation through His Son. And God will always forgive us when we have sincere hearts. But are you still wondering, *How can I move on after I've failed?* Let's turn to the Bible for the answer to that.

If anyone had a good reason to regret horrible things he'd done in his life, it was the apostle Paul. Before he met Jesus, Paul encouraged people to kill a righteous man named Stephen (Acts 7:59–8:1). He also played a major part in the persecution of Christians (Acts 9:1-2).

Can you imagine how Paul felt when Jesus brought him to his knees and gave him complete and unconditional forgiveness (Acts 9:1-5)? After that Paul knew he had to move on and serve God with his whole heart. No more wasted days! Oh, to be sure, Paul still probably had regrets and felt deep sorrow for his past actions. But he could also say:

> *Forgetting what is behind and straining toward what is ahead, I press on toward the goal to win the prize for which God has called me heavenward in Christ Jesus* (Philippians 3:13-14).

Friend, like Paul, you must make a few more choices. Choose to accept God's forgiveness for your past. And choose to remember His forgiveness every time you recall your past failures. Like Paul, you can choose to forget the past and press on. This is what will enable you to face each day and the coming years with excitement and joyful expectation of what God has prepared for you.

Your Heart Response

How often do people give you a second chance? Not very often, right? But God does! His forgiveness offers you a second... even a third or fourth or more...chances. You see, His forgiveness is limitless. All you have to do is come to Him with a *repentant* heart every time you sin.

But here's a word of caution: Your sorrow over the things you've done must be real. So be sure you examine your heart first. Ask, "What is my sorrow based on? Am I sorry for getting caught...or sorry for giving in to temptation? Am I sorry for disappointing people...or sorry for disappointing God?" When you approach God, go with a completely exposed heart. He will delight in giving you and your heart a thorough and loving cleansing.

And here's an encouraging thought about moving on: If you've strayed and taken the wrong path, you can start walking on a new and right path—God's path—any time. Even right now. And even if the consequences of your past actions continue, God can and will give you the grace and strength to do what is necessary to make things right and help you live with any consequences of your actions. You can do everything—including moving on, including turning your life around—through Christ who gives you strength (Philippians 4:13).

~~~ *Girls Helping Girls* ~~~

❀ Jot down several right choices Hannah finally made. What important corner has she turned?

❀ What comfort and words of encouragement would you give Hannah if you sat next to her in youth group?

❀ Of the verses shared in this chapter, which one meant the most to you, and why? How would you share this truth with Hannah?

❀ In what ways are you like Hannah? Do you need to take action regarding any bad choices you've made? What are they? What will you do first to turn your life around?

Want to Know More?
Check It Out!

✓ What do you learn about God's forgiveness from these verses?

Psalm 103:12—

Isaiah 1:18—

Matthew 26:28—

Acts 10:43—

1 John 1:9—

✓ It's been said that those who are forgiven much, forgive much. What do these verses say about your attitude in forgiving others?

Matthew 18:21-22—

Acts 7:59-60—

Ephesians 4:32—

Colossians 3:12-13—

God's Guidelines for Making Right Choices

✿ *Always remember you are known and blessed by God.* "Before I formed you in the womb I knew you, before you were born I set you apart" (Jeremiah 1:5).

✿ *Always remember you are loved by God, and His Son died for your sins.* "God demonstrates his own love for us in this: While we were still sinners, Christ died for us" (Romans 5:8).

✿ *Always remember you are accepted by God through His Son.* "Praise be to the God and Father of our Lord Jesus Christ, who has blessed us in the heavenly realms with every spiritual blessing in Christ" (Ephesians 1:3).

✿ *Always remember you are complete in Christ.* "In Christ all the fullness of the Deity lives in bodily form, and you have been given fullness in Christ, who is the head over every power and authority" (Colossians 2:9-10).

✿ *Always remember you are a work in progress and will one day be perfect.* "[Be] confident of this, that he who began a good work in you will carry it on to completion until the day of Christ Jesus" (Philippians 1:6).

Choice 13

A Fresh Start

*One thing I do: Forgetting what is behind and
straining toward what is ahead,
I press on toward the goal to win the prize
for which God has called me heavenward in Christ Jesus.*

PHILIPPIANS 3:13-14

Have you heard this statement: "Today is the first day of the rest of your life"? Well, that's exactly how Hannah felt as she sat on her bed Sunday afternoon. After her disastrous week she was amazed at how excited she was. And she was feeling good. Sundays are meant to be special, and this one truly was!

First of all, Hannah had been radically helped by Pastor Rick's teaching in youth group. What a jolt it had been...and then what a blessing. Her world had been rocked and changed.

And then Hannah had benefitted from the sermon given by the pastor during the regular worship service. In the past she'd always tuned out the senior pastor. She had a pretty long list of things to do during that time: doodle, clean out her purse, text her friends, and think about what she was going to wear to school on Monday. But today it was like she had new ears.

Wow! thought Hannah. *The sermon today was really awesome. It spoke to my heart. Pastor Porter was talking right to me. How did he know* exactly *what I needed to hear to help me follow through on my decision to start over and live for God?*

Your Life God's Way

Can you believe all that's happened to Hannah in only a few hours? Her entire life has shifted. She's heading in an entirely new, wonderful, and exciting direction. Hannah could hardly believe she was ready to commit to living God's way...and doing what He wanted her to do. She was shocked! Yet at the same time she was smiling, eagerly claiming her fresh start.

It's one thing to know what's right...and an entirely different thing to actually do and live what's right, to live life God's way, Hannah decided.

Yes, she had decided things were definitely going to be different—*way* different. Last week had been chaos. Hannah never wanted to experience another one like it. She was mulling over and praying about the new commitments she was making—choices that would express the life-changing decision she'd made in youth group.

And to doubly ensure that she didn't fall back into her old ways and habits, Hannah had asked Carol and Estelle to help her out. These two girls in her youth group also went to her school. They both agreed to stand with her, to pray for her, and to follow-up with her on her progress.

I think these two new friends will really help. They love God and want His best for me! Hannah decided. *I just hope Maria will respect the new me too.*

Getting Started

"Now, to get this fresh start going." Hannah looked at the stuff on her bed. "Bible...check. Personal journal and prayer notebook...check. Notes from Pastor Rick's class...check."

She was ready to take the pastor's advice and follow the principles he'd outlined for the group.

"Let me see. What did Pastor Rick say about living—really living—for Christ? Oh yeah, here it is. He gave us a checklist."

Daily Checklist for Christian Living

❀ *Start each day with God.* Spend time in God's Word. "Either sin will keep you from this Book, or this Book will keep you from sin."

❀ *Always include prayer.* Pray for yourself, your day, your family members, your attitude, your friends, and your walk with God.

❀ *Act like a child of God.* This includes how you dress and talk. Also how you treat your family.

❀ *Choose your friends carefully.* In the words of George Washington, "It is better to be alone than in bad company."

❀ *Do all things to the glory of God.* This includes school-work and activities.

❀ *Keep a cool, clear head when it comes to dating.* Don't be afraid to wait to date, to say no, to hold out for the right kind of person, and to involve your parents.

❀ *Stay pure.* It's better to be less popular and less experienced than to be sorry.

After Hannah read through Pastor Rick's daily checklist again, she knew how she would spend the rest of the day. Instead of talking on the phone, texting her friends, and spending time online, she would clean up her room. And she had homework to do. This evening she would spend time with her family… even with her younger brother and sister. And she'd look at these activities as honoring the Lord, not just pleasing herself, her parents, and her teachers. She might even get a head start on the Bible study for this week's meeting.

Hannah stopped and read Pastor Rick's checklist again. She made a mental note to go through her closet and choose her clothes for school tomorrow—something modest. And she definitely needed to decide when she was going to get up. Oh how she wanted to begin each new day with God! To spend time with Him and pray!

Oh, and she'd definitely be more careful and cautious with boys.

And…and…and…

Yes, Hannah was definitely making some right choices that would lead her in the right—and best!—direction—toward God and His way.

Your Heart Response

You, dear reader, have a wonderful and full life. These are exciting days for you! I know we haven't covered all the areas and issues of your life—that would be impossible. But I hope and pray you've glimpsed how important making right choices is...and that you *can* make the best choices each and every day. That's how you live life God's way—one choice at a time! Here's one of my favorite sayings:

> Every day is a little life,
> and your whole life is a single day repeated.

This means that each day is vitally important. Each day you can choose to...

❀ live for Christ

❀ live in an orderly environment

❀ live by walking in the Spirit

❀ live by making right choices

...or you can choose not to. To help you make the best choices, I've included a summary of the steps to right choices at the end of this chapter. Copy it, scan it, or tear it out and post it someplace where you'll see it often. The "7 Steps to Making Right Choices" is short and to the point. Refer to it as you start your day and again each time you're faced with one of your many choices. Put copies on your mirror and inside your locker door. Do whatever you have to do to use it. And why not share the list with your friends?

Put God's principles to work in your life. Ask Him to help you stayed committed to making the right choices that will create a better life for you and those around you. Think about the guidelines shared in this book and how you can live them out...beginning now. Experience what the apostle Paul meant when he declared: "To live is Christ" (Philippians 1:21).

As we end our together-journey, I want to tell you, my new

young friend, how proud I am of you for reading this book and living your commitment for Christ. God will bless your faithfulness as you trust in Him and follow Him with all your heart!

Elizabeth George

7 Steps to Making Right Choices

✺ *Stop.* Don't rush your decisions. "Fools rush in where angels fear to tread."[1]

✺ *Wait.* Evaluate your choices and options. It's better to miss an opportunity than get into something that might harm you or dishonor God.

✺ *Pray.* Talk to God. Tell Him you want to do the right thing and ask for His wisdom. He's promised to give it!

✺ *Search the Scriptures.* God's Word is your guidebook. Everything you need is there to help you make the best choices.

✺ *Ask for advice.* Ask someone who loves God if the choice you're about to commit to is the best option.

✺ *Make a decision.* In faith and with the assurance that you've done all you can humanly do, make your decision.

✺ *Act on your decision.* Follow through on your wise choice. And if more information comes to light later on, remember it's okay to go through these steps again.

Notes

Making the Right Choices

1. Neil S. Wilson, ed., *The Handbook of Bible Application* (Wheaton, IL: Tyndale House Publishers, Inc., 2000), pp. 86-87.
2. Elizabeth Prentiss, *Stepping Heavenward* (Amityville, NY: Calvary Press, 1993), p. 51.

Choice 1 — Ya Gotta Get Up!

1. "Teen Esteem," quoted in Roy B. Zuck, *The Speaker's Quote Book* (Grand Rapids, MI: Kregel Publications, 1997), p. 165.
2. Adapted from Derek Kidner, *The Proverbs* (Downers Grove, IL: InterVarsity Press, 1973), pp. 42-43.
3. John Piper, *Don't Waste Your Life* (Wheaton, IL: Crossway Books, 2003), backcover.

Choice 2 — Get into God's Word

1. Gwen Ellis and Sarah Hupp, *God's Words of Life for Teens* (Grand Rapids, MI: Inspirio, 2000), p. 29.

Choice 3 — Talk Things Over with God

1. Adapted from Elizabeth George, *A Young Woman's Call to Prayer* (Eugene, OR: Harvest House Publishers, 2005), pp. 25-33.
2. Joe White and Jim Weidmann, gen. eds., citing Nanci Hellmich, "A Teen Thing: Losing Sleep," *USA Today,* May 28, 2000 (USAToday.com), *Parent's Guide to the Spiritual Mentoring of Teens* (Wheaton, IL: Tyndale House Publishers, 2001), p. 447.
3. Adapted from Jim George, *The Bare Bones Bible Handbook for Teens* (Eugene, OR: Harvest House Publishers, 2008), p. 79.

Choice 4 — The Golden Rule Begins at Home

1. *Life Application Bible* (Wheaton, IL: Tyndale House Publishers, Inc., 1988), p. 1339.
2. Elizabeth George, *A Young Woman After God's Own Heart* (Eugene, OR: Harvest House Publishers, 2003), p. 99.
3. Elizabeth Prentiss, *Stepping Heavenward* (Amityville, NY: Calvary Press, 1993), p. 70.

Choice 5 — "I Have Nothing to Wear!"

1. Curtis Vaughan, gen. ed., *The Word—The Bible from 26 Translations*, quoting Charles B. Williams, *The New Testament. A Translation in the Language of the People* (Gulfport, MS: Mathis Publishers, Inc., 1993), p. 2273.
2. John MacArthur Jr., *The MacArthur New Testament Commentary—1 Timothy* (Chicago: Moody Press, 1995), pp. 80-81.

Choice 7 — What's That Coming Out of Your Mouth?

1. Gwen Ellis and Sarah Hupp, *God's Words of Life for Teens* (Grand Rapids, MI: Zondervan Corp., 2000), p. 103.
2. Gene A. Getz, *The Measure of a Woman* (Glendale, CA: Regal Books, 1977), p. 32.

Choice 8 — Choose the Road to Success

1. Adapted from Sterling W. Sill, cited in Paul Lee Tan, *Encyclopedia of 7700 Illustrations* (Winona Lake, IN: BMH Books, 1979), pp. 723-24.

Choice 10 — Date Without Regrets

1. Adapted from Elizabeth George, *Cultivating a Life of Character—Judges/Ruth,* a Woman After God's Own Heart® Bible study (Eugene, OR: Harvest House Publishers, 2002), p. 134.

2. Joe White and Jim Weidmann, gen eds., *Spiritual Mentoring of Teens* (Wheaton, IL: Tyndale House Publishers, 2001), p. 525.

3. *God's Words of Life for Teens* (Grand Rapids, MI: The Zondervan Corp., 2000), p. 33.

Choice 11 — Why's a Nice Girl Doing That?

1. Elizabeth George, "My Prayer for Purity," © 2009.

Choice 13 — A Fresh Start

1. Alexander Pope, "An Essay on Criticism," published in 1711.

Personal Notes

Personal Notes

Personal Notes

_____
_____
_____
_____
_____
_____
_____
_____
_____
_____
_____
_____
_____
_____
_____
_____
_____
_____
_____
_____
_____

Personal Notes

Personal Notes

_____

_____

_____

_____

_____

_____

_____

_____

_____

_____

_____

_____

_____

_____

_____

_____

_____

_____

Personal Notes

_____
_____
_____
_____
_____
_____
_____
_____
_____
_____
_____
_____
_____
_____
_____
_____
_____
_____
_____
_____
_____
_____

Personal Notes

_____

_____

_____

_____

_____

_____

_____

_____

_____

_____

_____

_____

_____

_____

_____

_____

_____

_____

_____

_____

_____

_____

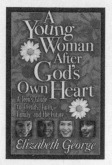

A Young Woman After God's Own Heart

Discover God's plan and purpose for your life! What does it mean to pursue God's heart in your everyday life? It means understanding and following God's perfect plan for your friendships, your faith, your family relationships, and your future. Bible teacher Elizabeth George reveals how you can…

- grow closer to God
- enjoy meaningful relationships
- make wise choices
- become spiritually strong
- build a better future
- fulfill the desires of your heart

Get caught up in the exciting adventure of a lifetime—become a woman after God's own heart!

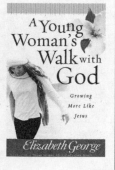

A Young Woman's Walk with God

~ Gold Medallion Award finalist ~

Travel with Jesus! Love, joy, peace, patience, kindness, goodness, faithfulness, gentleness, and self-control are qualities Jesus possessed—and He wants you to have them too! Bestselling author Elizabeth George takes you step by step through the fruit of the Spirit to help you get the most out of your life. By paying attention to your journey with God, you'll be able to…

- be positive as you interact with your family and friends
- have peace regardless of the pressures of school and relationships

❀ experience joy even when facing difficulties

❀ find the strength to come through on your commitments

❀ get control over bad habits

As you walk with Jesus your life will be more exciting and fulfilling every day…in every way.

A Young Woman's Call to Prayer

God wants to hear from you! He has given you an amazing gift—the ability to personally talk with Him every day! Through prayer, you can share with God your joys and triumphs, hurts and fears, and wants and needs, knowing that He cares about every detail of your life. Bestselling author Elizabeth George will help you…

❀ develop a stronger relationship with God

❀ set a regular time to talk to Him

❀ share sticky situations and special concerns with Him

❀ discover and live His will

❀ activate a heart that centers on Him

God is your forever friend—and He's always ready to talk with you! Experience the joy of knowing Him in a very real way through prayer.

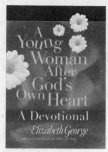

A Young Woman After God's Own Heart— A Devotional

God wants to encourage you each and every day! He has input that can change your day, take away your worries, and lift your hopes. In His amazing love, He cares about all the details of your life. In this pocket-sized devotional, bestselling author Elizabeth George shares ideas and thoughts to put you in touch with God and help you...

- ✻ live your faith
- ✻ let go of your worries
- ✻ hold out for the desires of your heart
- ✻ grow in beauty and confidence
- ✻ take your problems to God

This faith journey will fill your life with joy and purpose. Don't miss the incredible, life-changing journey to God's heart.

The Bare Bones Bible® Handbook for Teens

An awesome way to get to know your Bible! God wrote the Bible so that you could get to know Him and live a better life. But the Bible is a *big* book filled with *lots* of information. How can you ever get to know it and use it in your everyday life?

That's what *The Bare Bones Bible® Handbook for Teens* is all about. In just 10 minutes you can discover the key points of any book of the Bible. You'll learn...

- ✻ the big idea of each book
- ✻ the main people and events

❋ the important lessons for personal and spiritual growth

You'll be amazed at how much the Bible has to say about the things that matter most to you—your happiness, friends and family, home and school, and goals for the future.

A must-have guide for every teen and youth group!

A Young Man After God's Own Heart
~ Gold Medallion Award finalist ~

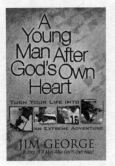

Experience the adventure of a lifetime! Pursuing God really *is* an adventure—one that can sometimes get extreme. Becoming a young man after God's own heart is a lot like climbing a mountain. You'll find all kinds of challenges on the way up!

But the awesome view at the top is well worth the trip. As you go higher and higher, you'll experience the thrill of knowing *real* success in life—the kind that counts with God. And it all starts by learning God's priorities for you, including...

❋ building your faith

❋ choosing the right kinds of friends

❋ getting along at home

❋ making wise choices about the future

❋ fighting the battle against temptation

Once you get started on the journey, you'll never be the same!

BIBLE STUDIES *for* BUSY WOMEN

A WOMAN AFTER GOD'S OWN HEART BIBLE STUDIES

Character Studies

Old Testament Studies

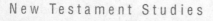

New Testament Studies

Elizabeth takes women step-by-step through the Scriptures, sharing wisdom she's gleaned from more than 30 years as a women's Bible teacher.

Embracing God's Grace
NEW
COLOSSIANS/PHILEMON
Elizabeth George

• MINUTE FOR BUSY WOMEN •

Elizabeth George can also be heard on the radio with her feature
"A Woman After God's Own Heart."

Books by Elizabeth George

- Beautiful in God's Eyes
- Beautiful in God's Eyes for Young Women
- Breaking the Worry Habit…Forever
- Finding God's Path Through Your Trials
- Following God with All Your Heart
- The Heart of a Woman Who Prays
- Life Management for Busy Women
- Loving God with All Your Mind
- Loving God with All Your Mind DVD and Workbook
- A Mom After God's Own Heart
- A Mom After God's Own Heart Devotional
- Moments of Grace for a Woman's Heart
- One-Minute Inspiration for Women
- Prayers to Calm Your Heart
- Quiet Confidence for a Woman's Heart
- Raising a Daughter After God's Own Heart
- The Remarkable Women of the Bible
- Small Changes for a Better Life
- Walking with the Women of the Bible
- A Wife After God's Own Heart
- A Woman After God's Own Heart®
- A Woman After God's Own Heart®— Daily Devotional
- A Woman's Daily Walk with God
- A Woman's Guide to Making Right Choices
- A Woman's High Calling
- A Woman's Walk with God
- A Woman Who Reflects the Heart of Jesus
- A Young Woman After God's Own Heart
- A Young Woman After God's Own Heart— A Devotional
- A Young Woman's Guide to Discovering Her Bible
- A Young Woman's Guide to Making Right Choices
- A Young Woman's Guide to Prayer
- A Young Woman Who Reflects the Heart of Jesus

Study Guides

- Beautiful in God's Eyes Growth & Study Guide
- Finding God's Path Through Your Trials Growth & Study Guide
- Following God with All Your Heart Growth & Study Guide
- Life Management for Busy Women Growth & Study Guide
- Loving God with All Your Mind Growth & Study Guide
- Loving God with All Your Mind Interactive Workbook
- A Mom After God's Own Heart Growth & Study Guide
- The Remarkable Women of the Bible Growth & Study Guide
- Small Changes for a Better Life Growth & Study Guide
- A Wife After God's Own Heart Growth & Study Guide
- A Woman After God's Own Heart® Growth & Study Guide
- A Woman's Call to Prayer Growth & Study Guide
- A Woman's High Calling Growth & Study Guide
- A Woman Who Reflects the Heart of Jesus Growth & Study Guide

Children's Books

- A Girl After God's Own Heart
- A Girl After God's Own Heart Devotional
- A Girl's Guide to Making Really Good Choices
- God's Wisdom for Little Girls
- A Little Girl After God's Own Heart

Books by Jim George

- 10 Minutes to Knowing the Men and Women of the Bible
- The Bare Bones Bible® Handbook
- The Bare Bones Bible® Handbook for Teens
- A Boy After God's Own Heart
- A Boy's Guide to Making Really Good Choices
- A Dad After God's Own Heart
- A Husband After God's Own Heart
- Know Your Bible from A to Z
- A Leader After God's Own Heart
- A Man After God's Own Heart
- A Man After God's Own Heart Devotional
- The Man Who Makes a Difference
- One-Minute Insights for Men
- A Young Man After God's Own Heart
- A Young Man's Guide to Discovering His Bible
- A Young Man's Guide to Making Right Choices

Books by Jim & Elizabeth George

- A Couple After God's Own Heart
- A Couple After God's Own Heart Interactive Workbook
- God's Wisdom for Little Boys
- A Little Boy After God's Own Heart

About the Author

Elizabeth George is a bestselling author whose passion is to teach the Bible in a way that changes women's lives. For information about Elizabeth's books or to sign up for her mailings, or to share how God has used this book in your life, please contact Elizabeth at:

www.ElizabethGeorge.com